MW01281948

All Things *pink*:

Bilateral Mastectomy & Me

By Sherri Coner

©2015 Sherri Coner. All rights reserved.

No part of this book may be reproduced, stored in a retrieval system, or transmitted by any means without the written permission of the author.

ISBN-13: 978-1517599607

ISBN-10: 1517599601

Because of the dynamic nature of the Internet, any web addresses or links contained in the book may have changed since publication and may no longer be valid. The views expressed in this work are solely those of the author.

DEDICATION

If you will soon lose your breasts to cancer, know that thousands of other breast cancer survivors don't even need to know your name to know your heart. We hold your hand in spirit. Every step of the way, we're with you. We are resilient. We are survivors. And you are, too. You are one of us.

Chapter One

I knew before the doctor called with the test results.

Yep, I did.

And for some weird reason, I kept it to myself.

It reminded me of trying on clothes in a dressing room but not looking in the mirror until the skirt was smoothed and the blouse was buttoned. That ritual was only to avoid eyeballing my cellulite under fluorescent lights. But with the test results, I suppose I was preparing myself to wear my diagnosis.

I needed time to smooth out the wrinkles before I showed anyone else what breast cancer looked like on me. I stood in front of the bathroom mirror, examining my reflection for the slightest changes. But I found nothing. No mysterious green warts popping up on my chest. No difference on my face except the red, puffy eyes and blotchy cheeks from crying a million tears. I reminded myself that no one could actually see breast cancer on me. That meant I didn't have to talk about it until there was no longer a way to avoid it.

I didn't look different. And yet everything was different.

Very few of my life steps have been planned. I just kind of got there, like running blindly toward a base on a ball field. One minute I am minding my own business, watching the game from the sidelines. But the next minute, I am on the run.

Every now and then, I get smashed in the face. Sometimes it's a financial smash. Sometimes it's a male-motivated smash. Most of the time, I never see it coming, either. I have the observational skills of a cow.

Anyway, the smash in the face from breast cancer occurred in October 2013, the month for my annual mammogram. Every single year I secretly wondered if it was now my turn to "catch it." Like a cold.

Breast cancer.

I even role-played in my head about how brave I would be if I found myself facing such a scary diagnosis. Like thousands of women, my life was touched by breast cancer long before my own diagnosis. The first time was in my twenties, when one of my maternal aunts underwent a bilateral mastectomy. Her fear, moments before she was taken to surgery, has stayed on my heart for nearly thirty years. At the time, I had no idea how to even begin to process what it might be like for my aunt or any woman to lose her breasts to cancer. What registered most for me was how my aunt sobbed on the gurney and how deeply I felt her pain.

After the surgery, she lost her hair to chemotherapy, and for a while, she also lost that sweetness in her eyes. When she showed me the scars on her breastless chest, I dropped my eyes. I felt sick and so very sorry for her. It was an experience that has never faded. As time passed, two more female relatives were diagnosed. One lost her breasts, and the second one won the pink-ribbon lottery by undergoing a lumpectomy and radiation.

My breasts were dense, which made it difficult sometimes for the radiologist to get a clear read on the tissues. Because of that, mammograms occasionally had to be repeated, which sent me into a tearful frenzy. Even though I tried not to live that constant feeling of Russian roulette, I remained conscious of the fact that breast cancer was definitely hanging out in the breasts of my female family members. Of course, many women who are diagnosed with this disease have absolutely no family history. Breast cancer is a sneaky villain.

Sometimes there's just no way to guess whether a woman will

safely keep her breasts on her body for all of her life. And for some reason, my fiftieth birthday felt like it shoved me even further into a danger zone. I felt much more vulnerable to it.

I had planned to leave Florida to do several book signings and a radio interview in Indiana a few days after undergoing my October mammogram. For several weeks, I had focused on that trip north, hoping it would provide the extra push I needed for my career. For as long as I can remember, I have been in love with storytelling. For as long as I can remember, I have also dreamed about staying at home in my pajamas, to write books laced with humor and powerful messages for women. My heart was so full of hope and excitement about the trip, not just about my books but also about seeing so many people that I loved so dearly.

In an effort to avoid the usual pre-mammogram nervousness the morning of my screening, I thought about the weather as I drove to the doctor's office. When I got my boobs squashed in Indiana, winter was in the air by October. Most of the leaves had already shared their brightest colors and fallen from the trees. Here in Florida, October might as well be June, with lush green grass and lazy palm trees, flowers blooming. There was nothing bad about comparing the two. Just different. It was a boring subject, but at least it delayed my freak-out session until I walked into the doctor's waiting room and immediately felt nauseated. While I waited for my turn, I attempted to read a book I brought along.

But it was nearly impossible to concentrate.

When my name was called, I stood in that tiny room with the monster mammogram machine and the drill was the same. Remove the monster minimizer bra. Plop the boobs on the ice-cold tray. Hold my breath. Don't move. In my case, stop imagining that any minute, a nipple would pop off from the squashing and ping-pong around on the colorless walls. A few minutes later, the test was over. I wrestled back into my bra, buttoned my blouse and made a list in my head for the grocery store stop on my way home.

But then time stopped.

And I can't even explain to you how much I mean that. I've heard that saying plenty of times. But until that day, I never understood that it could be a real feeling. Everything in my world just froze up, stopped breathing and being. It happened when the radiologist asked to speak to me. My love for words and all of my plans for the trip to Indiana ran for cover in the back of my brain the very moment I saw the expression on his face. As I followed him into a small dark room, I felt sick again. My hands were clammy. My vision was foggy. For some reason, even then, I knew this little meeting was not about a repeat mam for dense breast tissue.

After nicely offering me a seat, which I did not accept, the radiologist calmly sat down in a swivel chair and pointed at a few TV screens, my mammogram results from different angles. He then pointed specifically at the freckled white dots on one of the screens. While I looked over his shoulder, he explained in a monotone voice that calcification often develops in the breasts of women over fifty. That it is normal for that to happen. But while he spoke, my sixth sense quietly kicked into fifth gear. Had I refused to sit beside the nice radiologist because I might need to sprint out of here to escape this awful moment? I imagined myself as a little girl with my fingers plugging my ears, singing silly songs and stomping my feet. Doing whatever was necessary to avoid the words I wasn't yet brave enough to hear. That nasty history of breast cancer in the family burned in my stomach.

"If the calcifications begin to cluster, that can be a problem," he said, while never taking his eyes off the screen. "It might be a breast cancer problem."

Those words, "breast cancer problem," felt like a hot iron on my chest. I snarled my hands into shaky knots before hiding them

4

behind my back. I could not think of anything to say. I could not find my voice. I stood there, mute and nauseated.

"Yes," the radiologist continued. "Clustered calcifications can be associated with breast cancer. So we will want to do a diagnostic mammogram. Can you be here tomorrow?"

Show up again tomorrow? This situation was quickly turning into the nightmare I have secretly carried with me for so many years. In my head, I tried to believe the mammogram was only being repeated because the reading was unclear. In my heart, I was screaming, "This guy knows I have it. He's just going through the formalities. Oh my God, it's here. I have it."

"Can you?" His voice sliced through the fog that was already forming in my mind.

What? My mind tried to re-boot. What was he saying? I was watching his mouth move. But I could not connect with his words. I felt like I was under water. Drowning slowly.

"Can you be here tomorrow?" He asked again.

Yes. I just nodded my head because my throat was closing up. Yes. Tomorrow.

Somehow I found enough composure to leave the dark room without tripping over anything and also without saying one single word to the radiologist.

"He probably thinks I can't talk," I thought to myself as my trembling hand found the exit door. I thought about turning around to say, "By the way, mister, I can talk. Boy can I talk." But the sassy moment faded. "Who cares if he doesn't think I can talk? I don't want to talk, anyway. What I really want is to stand here and scream my head off."

With shaky fingers, I took the appointment card from the receptionist. I don't remember what I said or if I said anything to her. I don't know how I made it from the office to my car. My legs were like jelly. I started my car and reminded myself that nothing was conclusive. I held onto one word from the radiologist's mouth. And that word was *might*. Calcification *might* be a breast cancer problem.

That was all.

But wasn't that enough?

Twice on the way home, I was nearly involved in accidents with other drivers. Horns honked. One guy flipped me off when I drifted across two lanes of traffic, not even bothering to check my rearview mirror. On another day, I would have reacted with something bratty, like maybe blowing kisses in his direction. But on this day, I couldn't care less. I was oblivious to anything else in the entire world except calcifications.

"Stop it," I hissed at myself as a wave of tears took my breath. "There's no time for you to lose your damn mind. Grow up, why don't you? And deal with this."

After parking the car, I stumbled up the steps to the messy back porch of my tiny beach house. I reminded myself that yes, I was definitely awake. This was my address. That was my pile of notes on top of the table where I write. Yes. I am in this moment. This is real. I traded my skirt and blouse for a T-shirt and panties and returned to the porch with my laptop for a crash course in breast calcification. In my research, I discovered that my odds for having non-cancerous calcification was actually pretty impressive.

But then again, I have not led a very lucky life.

"Maybe this will be my streak of luck," I whispered. "Maybe I can duck the monster."

After a sleepless night, I showed up the next morning for the diagnostic mammogram, which is much like an MRI. My entire body shook as I removed my bra. Held my breath. Prayed in my head. But once again, the moment I was clothed, I was face-to-face with another radiologist. And once again, calcification was the hot topic of the day. He traced areas on the screen with his finger. This time, more words were added to the conversation: "two masses in the right breast."

"Damn it," I thought. "It's looking more and more like I'm headed toward hell. And there's absolutely nowhere to run."

That business about two masses obviously trumped *might*, which was yesterday's favorite word.

The cards were starting to stack against me. Two bad mammograms. Clustered calcification. Two masses in the right breast.

My legs shook as I once again stood at the reception desk. Now breast biopsies were scheduled. I couldn't think of anything to hold onto. Nothing. I was certain that I had "it." But I wasn't very sure at all that I could face any of this. I was so afraid — so deeply afraid, that for a few seconds, I didn't even notice that I was holding my breath. Maybe I was holding my breath because it is impossible to scream and curse and sob when you do. Who knows. My heart was pounding in my ears. I felt dizzy, or intoxicated maybe, by an enormous feeling of helplessness. I realized that I needed to somehow get hold of my fear. Grab it. Tame it. Maybe then I could more clearly think through this situation.

Shaking, I climbed into the driver's seat to head home. "Okay, God," I whispered. "I'm officially losing it."

I sat there for a few minutes without putting the key in the ignition. Sat there, staring out the window, trying to decide if I needed to stick my head out the car door and puke my head off. Trying to decide why my chest suddenly felt like it was full of ice. I wasn't bawling hysterically. I wasn't necessarily thinking about anything in particular, either. I think now that I was in shock. That my mind was on overload, brought on by two bad mams and two masses in my right breast.

Eighteen months earlier, I relocated alone from Indiana to

Southwest Florida. I made the decision after a third divorce and a third surgery for arthritis. Though I have some family members scattered in the area, I decided not to call them. Calling my son and daughter-in-law in Indiana or anyone else was also out of the question. Nope. I wouldn't tell anyone anything until I knew something for sure. I did not have the energy to talk about what I was going through, especially when I did not have a clear diagnosis. I did not have the heart to sprinkle drama on anyone else's life. And I would never scare my kid without good reason.

When I felt like I could focus enough to drive home, I started the car and drove slowly. That's unheard for a chick like me, and I have the speeding tickets to prove it. But on that day, I felt weighed down by fear and sadness, grief and a deep hurting, aching feeling.

Later that evening, I realized that I was playing a little game in my head by holding on tight to the fact that no one had officially made a diagnosis. Part of my mind decided that I had some mental wiggle room. I tried to tell myself that my heart was freaked out by the family history and those damn calcifications. My head tried its best to tell my heart to shut the hell up.

But my heartbeat moved into my ears. You have it. You have it. You have it.

It was such an odd state of mind, a split between the head and the heart.

My head said, "No one has told you that you absolutely have breast cancer."

My heart responded quickly with, "Come on, Sherri. No one has to tell you. As scary as it is, you already know."

My armor, the stuff I have always prided myself for wearing through any kind of crisis, was definitely beat to hell. That night, I fell apart. In the midst of my big meltdown, I tried to remind myself that I had always had a plan for breast cancer. That if it became part of my story, I would handle it well. But I wasn't handling it. Not at all.

I didn't put up much of a fight. Instead, I surrendered to the fear and spent hours on the shower floor. With my knees up and my face buried in my arms, the water beat down on my back until it ran cold. I stayed there, waiting for the water heater to kick in and bring another blast of hot water. I was too exhausted for anything else. That sentence — "Two masses in the right breast" — echoed in my head. Because I live alone, there was no one around to say things like, "Whatever happens, we will face it together" and "Let's pray for the best. But know that wherever you land with this, you can get through it." I went all the way to that fuzzy place involving fear and imagination. I wondered if breast cancer had already had a big party all over my body. Maybe I was dying. What did I need to do to prepare to die?

I talked to God a lot that night.

I never asked Him to take away the breast cancer.

But I sure did question whether I could take this new curve in my road, especially since my path was already filled with the boulders and debris of my past. The humiliating divorce was only a little part of where my energy had gone. I had also gone through surgery to replace two crumbled discs in my neck with titanium plates. I was still dealing with neuropathy from waiting ten months to secure health insurance so I could have the neck surgery. I moved away from Indiana, leaving behind lots of people I have known and loved all of my life. Only three months earlier, I finished injections and physical therapy for a nasty flare-up with arthritis. The list of ways my ass had been kicked in the last four years was endless.

And now I had breast cancer? What the hell?

"God, I promise I will take my turn," I wailed. "But please, please can't I wait until I feel stronger? Please, can't I have a chance to get myself better prepared? I feel too weak for this. I feel too sad and scattered. Where am I supposed to pull courage from, when I feel so empty?"

When I finally stepped out of the shower, the sun was coming up. I had forgotten to get a towel, and I dripped my way out of the bathroom, naked. For some reason, I stopped in the doorway of the guest bedroom. Between the two mammograms and the scheduled biopsy, I realized that I had not packed one single item for the trip north. In that moment, my heart reminded me that I already knew I would not board the airplane. I would not be present for book signings. I would miss the radio interview. I would not see my son and daughter-in-law. I would not be anywhere I planned to be in Indiana.

I would be right here.

Dealing with breast cancer.

All of the next day, I felt like I was suffocating. By midafternoon, I realized that I needed oxygen from somewhere. So I contacted Susie Johnson, a woman I only knew from Facebook -- a woman who had undergone a mastectomy a year or so ago. When I poured out the information, two bad mammograms and a scheduled biopsy for the following day, it was the first time I felt what the words sounded like when they left my mouth: It felt like I was strangling to death.

Susie cried for me.

And she cried with me.

We have never even met. And yet this woman immediately became my lifeline. She explained what to expect during the breast biopsy. She promised that once the procedure was over, the pain would end. From Susie's explanation, it sounded like I would physically be able to drive myself home afterward. And that was all I needed to know. I did not want to tell anyone anything until I had a diagnosis. It was such a strange feeling. I knew it inside, yet I was still hoping for a loophole. Still looking for a miracle. Still waiting for a radiologist to shake my hand and say, "Boy, that was a close one! We really thought you might have breast cancer. But you're fine!"

I have known for a long, long time that as soon as you can laugh about something awful, you can survive it. For nearly nine years, I wrote a weekly humor column for an Indiana newspaper, and my readers frequently reminded me of that truth. Everyone needs a laugh. Lots of times, laughter is necessary just to make it through a difficult day. Aging body parts used to really freak me out, so I wrote about this dilemma in my newspaper columns. I made fun of the changes in my anatomy by naming my large, floppy breasts Tiff and Alex. My lone ovary got a name, too: Helen.

But the possibility of hearing that I had breast cancer was not even close to humorous. How could I survive the serious stuff of breast cancer when being a smartass is my best coping skill? What would life be like if I lost Tiff and Alex?

My breasts?

My breasts?

Exhaustion set in again like a heavy blanket. I was beat up by the stress of undergoing two mammograms with bad results. And now, I needed to rally for the moment when a huge frigging needle would be drilled into one of my saggy old boobs. More than anything, I just wanted to curl into the fetal position and never come out from under the blankets.

When I got off the phone with Susie, I did try to hide. I tried to just go to bed and stay there until I had to face the biopsies. But once again, my damn brain would *not* shut the hell up. So I jerked off the covers and threw the pillows and stomped through the house trying to decide how to get through the time between that moment and the breast biopsies the next morning. I sat in my rocking chair on the screened porch and tried to clear my head.

"Obviously, you survived every single shitstorm in your life," I told myself. "So why do you doubt whether you can do this? Of course you can do it. You can do it just as soon as you stop acting like a big sissy ass about it."

I also thought about the fact that God never sends a struggle unless He wants us to do something with it, whether it's to learn lessons or teach others through our own pain. Ultimately I believe that He wants us to do something brave and beautiful with what we learn and how we heal. So I decided not to keep my secret. Even though it was scaring me so badly that I couldn't talk about it just yet, I would write about it. If the biopsy results confirmed what I already knew to be true, I would be as transparent as possible. I would take the power away from an issue that terrifies all women. And along the way, I would try harder to find something funny about it, just so I could keep moving.

Here is my first blog post:

Nov. 5, 2013

A diagnostic mammogram was scheduled for last Thursday. Immediately after the radiologist read the results, biopsies were scheduled.

I will admit that my stomach whispered to me ..."Uh oh ... you could be in some deep shit here, chickie."

Only 10 percent of testing on calcification clusters comes back with the big C word attached. That's pretty good odds.

I reminded myself that after all these years of loving that big vast ocean, I have been stung only once by a jellyfish ... and it was this past summer.

So I showed up for biopsies.

During this procedure, you must lie flat on your stomach with the suspicious boob dropped through a hole in the exam table.

Then the table is elevated so the doctor can work on your hanging boob with the same approach of a guy changing the oil in your car.

I found that to be pretty funny ...

Well, it was funny until it hurt like hell.

I told the (male) doctor that he was killing me. He responded with, "That shouldn't hurt. I numbed your breast."

I fired back with, "Why don't we trade places? You stick your scrotum in the hole. I will stick a needle through it. And then I will let you know whether or not it should hurt."

The nurses died laughing. The doctor ... not so much.

Soon after that, nothing was funny to me anymore. And I asked God to please let me faint.

But He never did. And it might have been because I was a smartass to the doctor only a few minutes earlier.

When I left the office, I was proud of myself for surviving the mutilation without a meltdown (at least not a public one). I was happy that I kept all the nastiness a secret.

This evening, after the office closed, my doctor called me ... not her assistant ... the doctor ...

I have it.

Right breast.

Better known as Alex ... Tiff's best friend.

Cancer.

I think I was stunned. And yet I wasn't shocked at all. My heart already knew it. But here it was. Truth.

"I have breast cancer?" I thought. "Those words don't go in my mouth. Do they?"

13

I am not the same person I was this morning, gingerly placing an ice pack on poor old bruised up Alex ... that biopsy was hell on my poor old boob.

I have breast cancer.

Like other women in my family.

Thank you, God, that I don't have a daughter to worry about ...

Who knows what is ahead.

I still have to meet with the surgeon. I still have to hear some things I probably do not want to hear. I have been through some other times in my life when I sure as hell did not want to show up and deal with the bad stuff.

But I will show up ... no matter how afraid I might be.

I can do this. ... In fact, I will do this to the best of my ability.

I have to hold on to knowing that everything will be exactly as it is meant to be ...

I just need to show up and trust and remember to breathe. God always takes care of me ... especially when I am too tired or too scared or too overwhelmed to take care of myself.

Chapter Two

For several days after undergoing the biopsies, my breast was all bruised up like she had been on the losing end of a cat fight. I couldn't wear a bra and kept an ice pack smashed against the biopsy site, to reduce the swelling. Other than the throbbing boob, I don't remember a lot about those first days and weeks after the diagnosis. I wish I could say that I sprang into action and got busy preparing to meet breast cancer head-on. But the truth is that I puddled under the diagnosis. Literally.

Maybe it happened because I was already so worn out with my life. The reasons don't really matter. The truth is that I turned into a snotty mess on the floor. Sometimes it felt almost like an out-of-body existence.

I remember sitting on the porch, taking in a shaky breath and practicing how to tell my son before I dialed his number. But I have no idea when I called him. I can't recall much of the conversation, either. I intended to fake my way through that phone call. Yes, my sweet boy is a grown man. But I wanted him to feel safe. I especially wanted him to think I had my act together. My ducks in a row. My plan intact for how I would tackle breast cancer. During that call, I tried to sound like everything was under control. Who knows if I actually accomplished the goal. I also dreaded having that conversation with my editor, Elaine. A few months earlier, she lost her best friend to breast cancer.

I hated to bring that pain back to Elaine's hurting heart. But I had to tell her that my engagements in Indiana had to be canceled. I have no clue when I called her. I have no idea what was said.

Melissa, the owner of a boutique in Brownsburg, Indiana, chose not to cancel the event. Instead, she displayed my books for customers, and the women raised money for breast cancer research. Women so beautifully stand together during times like these. They reminded me that something good could come from something that was choking me to death. My friend Rhonda canceled another engagement for me. I knew I could not make that call. Not without sobbing.

And then something very strange happened.

For the first time in my entire life, I realized that I could not talk.

I had already endured the weirdness of keeping the mammograms and biopsies top secret. That's definitely not me. I am an open book, the type who talks about vaginal infections in the produce aisle with women I've never met. I am the chick who blabs for hours on the phone. I love stories. I love to connect with other people. I wanted so badly to respond to the tearful voicemails and the beautifully written emails and Facebook posts from friends and readers. But I could not talk. My voice got lost in my throat and fell in between millions of tears. I couldn't do anything except remind myself to breathe.

All kinds of awful thoughts buzzed around in my head. There was no "off" switch. And because it got down to self-preservation, I turned all the way inside of myself. It felt a lot like I dove into the deep pocket of my favorite flannel robe.

I did not want to come out.

Ever.

I felt shell-shocked.

I felt weighted by every single thought that stomped its way through my exhausted mind.

This blog post better explains where my head was, 24 hours

into the diagnosis of breast cancer.

I am in a cocoon.... I have rolled up inside myself and settled in.

From the looks of things, I might be in here for a little while ...

I do not yet know how to have breast cancer.

I just can't talk about it right now.

I can't talk at all.

I can't talk because a million tears start to choke me to death. I have cried all day, For heaven's sake, I am crying when I don't even realize it ...

I am a big wrinkled mess of bawling snot and bad hair and no sleep. I am the commercial for how NOT to take on breast cancer. ha

Late this evening I rode my bike because I will do that when I can, just like I will walk the beach and write and laugh and talk (eventually I will talk ... but who knows when).

Yes I will do all of that and lots more ...

Breast cancer is not everything, you know. And I don't plan on giving it a damn thing that I am not forced to give.

Anyway, I rode my bike to the back bay, sat on the dock and had myself another little meltdown ...

I don't understand why I am crying so much ...

I already know that I am not drivin' this bus ... I already know that I will accept whatever is ahead of me. And I already know that I am strong enough to do whatever I have to do.

I am very strong.

I am the chick you want on your team ... because I hang on.

Well, I hang on to everything except asshole husbands.

I am sitting on the porch now, listening to the wind ... and blowing my nose for the eight hundredth time.

Tomorrow I meet with the breast surgeon ... with my snot rags in my fists, I will show up.

And maybe I will find my voice by then.

November 2013:

It has been a very long first week with breast cancer. It's been a snotty week, too.

I've done so much crying, I feel like I've been battered by a storm filled with jagged edges and so many feelings.

But I also feel like I have been hugged and loved a lot, through some very scary moments, by women I have known forever and women I have never met.

On Facebook, especially, I have received so many kind words. So many raw, honest stories from other women who have been where I am going.

Hearing my son's silence on the other end of the phone, when I told him ... that barely audible, "I'm scared, Ma," was definitely a time this week when I lost my breath and couldn't find it for a while.

I want him to trust that I am strong.

Don't be afraid. I am not leaving you.

November 2013:

This morning, the nurse navigator called. Her job is to keep me on the right path with all the right doctors. I lost it a little bit. But I managed to recover and grab hold of some sanity before it was too late.

We talked about the breast cancer history in my family and the possible need for BRCA testing. But I'm not so sure that I should spend my energy hoping that I test negative for the gene mutation.

Definitely, it took all week to get in the mood to tackle this new challenge.

But I'm here now. And I need the details so I can make a plan.

Instead of beating myself to death with "what if," I have made a new goal. I simply want to stay in each moment. Just move from moment to moment until I get some focus.

Chapter Three

After one week of knowing, I was still searching for a way to carry breast cancer around with me. My hands were already full of so many other issues. I didn't know how to take on something that seemed so sinister. I imagined that if breast cancer were tangible, it had to weigh at least a thousand pounds. It had to be deep black in color and covered with spikes and thorns. It had to be filled with black widow spiders, rats and any other something that causes a woman to fly from zero to hysteria. On the morning of my first appointment with an oncologist, I stood in front of the bathroom mirror, still trying to believe it, trying to add makeup to my swollen red eyes.

"You have to see an oncologist today because you have cancer," I said to my reflection. "You do. You have breast cancer. It's true and you'd better get used to it."

It was still so difficult to believe that after all the years of worrying about it, dodging it and hoping to always fly under the radar to avoid it, breast cancer caught up with me. It had me around the neck, and I tried to feel like I had some control by conversing with myself about the course of treatment.

"If I have to lose my breasts, that's better than undergoing chemotherapy," I said softly as I dusted or washed dishes or swept off the porch. "If I can have a lumpectomy and radiation, I will feel so lucky. But only if I don't also have to take tamoxifen for five years."

I asked my Aunt Barb to accompany me that day to see the doctor. I had not slept since the diagnosis. I didn't trust myself to hold the mind fog at bay. I was not confident at all in my ability to

21

take in everything the oncologist had to say. Armed with a pad of paper and a pen, she and I walked into the small waiting room where all of the other women were older than me. They all had a man beside them. And that stung my heart so much that tears filled my eyes. That's when it hit me. I would go through this alone. Even though I had my sweet aunt, other family members and my girlfriends, too, there would be no intimate partner beside me. No one to tell me that I was loved for so many more reasons than my breasts. I sat on the edge of the chair, feeling vulnerable and embarrassed that I had no husband. I'm not sure why that feeling came over me. I have never been the type to think that I need a person with a penis to feel worthy. Maybe I thought everyone in the waiting area would whisper about me. "Look at her. She has cancer and nothing else."

That isn't true, of course. I have lots of other things in my life. But whether they admit it or not, a lot of women — and men, too — judge middle-aged women who are not married. They start trying to guess what the problem is. They come up with their own labels, such as "frigid" or "gold digger," "alcoholic" or "crazy." Some married women don't want to be friends with a single woman because they fear the single friend will try to sleep with their husband. I don't want married friends who would even entertain the thought that I would do something like that to them. They can keep their nasty paranoia and their adolescent drama all to themselves. I don't want any part of stupid shit like that.

In my head, I conjured up a big visual. I saw myself standing on top of the outdated magazines on the waiting room coffee table to explain to the judgmental patients that I don't have a husband because I happen to be an ass magnet.

"I can't seem to help it," I would say loudly. "I draw sociopaths. That's why I don't have a man holding my hand and whispering sweetly in my ear. Okay? Any other concerns? If not, then why don't all of you just mind your own damn business?"

When my name was called, I was thankful to see that my oncologist, someone I never wanted to need in my life, was upbeat and positive. My diagnosis, ductal carcinoma, was caught at an early stage. This fact made me a perfect candidate for a lumpectomy and some rounds of radiation. Of course, that treatment option fit right into my private plan of best options. I felt like I had won the big, you-can-keep-your-boobs prize. I left the doctor's office absolutely overjoyed. My aunt and I stopped at the grocery so I could break my no-sugar diet.

I practically skipped into the bakery area to buy a fat chocolate doughnut as big as my head and celebrate the fact that my boobs weren't going anywhere. For some reason, I spluttered my great news at the sweet cashier. Her name was Julie, and she shared with me that her best friend was a breast cancer survivor. Julie even showed me a tattoo in her friend's honor, on her leg: a perfectly tatted pink ribbon. We had this weird, instant connection. I still stop in the store to say hello, and we are friends on Facebook.

But then, my world turned upside down again.

No sooner had my aunt said goodbye and left me at home alone with my kazillion-calorie doughnut, feeling like I just dodged a bullet the size of Texas, than the oncologist called. When he told me earlier that a lumpectomy was a great possibility, it was before he saw my family history. A decision about the course of treatment should be delayed until I could undergo genetic testing. If I happened to test positive for the BRCA gene, my chances for developing breast cancer again would skyrocket.

After I hung up the phone, I realized that my heart and head were in cahoots. I wonder now if they were always a tag team and I was just too screwed up to notice. Even though the option of lumpectomy and aggressive rounds of radiation were still on the table, something began to tap at my sense of self. Something continuously began to whisper, "It doesn't matter if you think for a while that you are a candidate for lumpectomy. You already know it, girlie. You will be losing your breasts to cancer."

This post was written after the visit with the oncologist.

I fell asleep around 9:30 p.m. Woke up at 2 a.m. and sat outside. No crying. Just a lot of thinking.

I went back to bed around 6 a.m. and got up with the sun.

I started to wash a sink full of dishes, which I had purposefully left there since yesterday so my mind had something to keep it busy ... and all of a sudden, I am sobbing on the kitchen floor.

I have absolutely no control over my emotions. I am back in my cocoon so I can safely have these unscheduled tearful moments without an audience.

I need to get myself together. I don't want to show up for genetic testing looking like I need a padded room.

These tears feel like a big wave in my chest. They take over and I feel like I might drown.

I don't understand why I am acting this way. I already know the options. If the test is negative, I can choose lumpectomy and radiation. If it isn't, I will lose my breasts. And I will live through that, just like my aunts have.

I feel like a baby. My situation could be a zillion times more serious.

But these tears...these big, hot tears are uncontrollable.

Maybe my soul is crying. Not just for me but for every other woman who faces breast cancer.

I must remind myself that I am still strong, even if my soul is crying.

This is the post from the day I underwent genetic testing.

Nov. 14, 2013

When I found the building, my heart jiggled in my chest. This is my new club ... the women's cancer center.

Inside, I am overwhelmed by evidence of the big C. Women with no hair. Women with flat chests. Women snuggled in the arms of loving husbands.

I could not have counted on any of my exes to be emotionally available to me during this life crisis ... not one.

I decide, right there in the midst of all kinds of nasty cancer issues, that I finally know what I would need from a man. But I don't have a man ... and I am sad and thankful for that, all in the same moment.

I stand in the back of the elevator with my head down and play with the tassel tie on my blouse. I force my eyes to memorize the way my breasts look under my clothing.

I think about taking pictures of my chest. I think about how it will feel if I have to lose my breasts. I wish with all of my heart that I had one photograph of myself nursing my child.

But when you are young, you never think about a day when your breasts will be cut off.

Two other women step into the elevator, and I try my best to keep my head down. I take some deep breaths and swallow those very familiar sobs that line up in my throat. When they step out at the second floor, one of the women smiles warmly and squeezes my hand.

I cry all the way to the third floor. I cannot talk. I cannot stand to be touched. All of my body is curled up in pain.

I find the doctor's office. It's decorated nicely with white leather couches and lavender walls. When I approach the receptionist to say my name, those tears rush forward and drown me. I absolutely cannot speak. I can't breathe. I am so embarrassed.

The harder I try to get myself under control, the crying only gets worse. The receptionist offers a warm expression of, "It's okay." But it's not okay at all with me that I am absolutely not finding a way to grab hold of my damn self.

Finally, I manage my name. I am led down the hall to do the genetic test. I have no idea what to expect, but I am pleasantly surprised. All I need to do is slosh Scope in my mouth for 20 seconds and spit into a test tube. After repeating this two more times, the test is over.

I am so thankful to be alone in the elevator that I almost start crying again.

In the lobby, I walk past a gift shop called Cookies. I see pink everything in there. Wigs and scarves. Books. Statues. I don't step inside. Nope, I can't. I just can't.

I get in line at a snack bar so I can buy a bottled water and swallow Excedrin for a blinding headache. I feel weird. I feel like all the other women are looking at me, sizing me up. Does she have ovarian cancer? Breast cancer? Both?

I decide that I am just losing my damn mind. If they are looking at me at all, it's probably because my eyes are red swollen slits, from bawling, bawling, bawling.

I am surprised at myself. I have spent my life reaching out to other women. But I cannot open my mouth to ask anyone any of the questions racing through my mind. I cannot open my mouth without a big rush of tears ...

From the cancer center, I head north to meet my parents for lunch.

They drove from Indiana to Florida, to be here for me. And in a way, I don't want them here.

I don't want them to worry. I don't want to cause them any pain. I promise myself that for the lunch time, I will try my best to keep my shit together. Whatever it takes, I will do it. I want them to see me as strong and capable. I don't want to be viewed as the daughter with breast cancer. And I certainly don't want to be viewed as the daughter with breast cancer who is now cracking up.

I surprise myself with how well I pull off the lunch visit. Emotionally, I pull myself way, way, way back ... so far away that I can barely hear myself say to them that it looks like I will need to do bilateral mastectomy. I say it as if I am talking about a new battery for my car.

I don't want them to ask why I think I have to do a mastectomy. I will not reveal that my intuition is telling me this information. They will flip out and decide I need shock treatments while I also go through breast cancer.

It is important to plant the seed. I want them to know that everything is headed that direction.

But I don't want to send them over the proverbial cliff, so I fake my way through the conversation. I don't want to freak out in front of them. They might insist that I return to Indiana for treatment. They might demand that I stay with them. I don't want any of that. I only feel safe alone, where I can cry my face off when I feel like it. I can't stand to be around anyone right now.

When I get home, I immediately fall asleep on the couch.

Everything takes so much effort right now ... everything.

Chapter Four

Waiting for the results of genetic testing was nothing less than excruciating. The doctor's office said it could be two weeks before I heard anything. I wondered how in the world I could possibly survive the stress. It consumed me. I couldn't sleep and had no appetite.

By the way, that seemed to be the only perk of my situation. I dropped weight like crazy and started thinking that the breast cancer diet was much more effective than all three of my divorce diets put together. Rather twisted way to look at things. But I grabbed at every chance I had to be sarcastic. Maybe I had to have breast cancer. But on the sunny side, I had a waist again.

I posted my thoughts on Facebook and on my blog. But I still avoided answering my phone. I didn't want to hear tears in friends' voices. I didn't want to hear, "I'm so sorry, Sherri." I didn't want to hold my breath until I was dizzy, trying way too hard to keep my bruised emotions under control when they were clearly so out of control.

For those same reasons, I also did not want company. I only felt safe from myself when I was alone. And by safe, I mean that I found comfort in sitting alone with my crying spells. But then I have always been that way. You know how an injured dog takes off to hide alone in the bushes? That's me. I handle everything better if I can just be left alone. Then I don't have to feel guarded about my emotions. In this case, my hysterical mood swings involved lots of mucus smeared all over my face. I never knew when the water works would erupt like a tsunami. And I damn sure did not want an audience.

My mind wandered all over the place, from whether I would lose my breasts, to the painful crevices of my past. I thought about my awful divorces and my bad judgment. I started to beat myself to death for every single mistake I have ever made. And that was a lot of beating, you know. That list of mistakes is a long one. I spent hours analyzing my deep, self-destructive need to feel loved and safe — and how my self-esteem was repeatedly dragged through gravel in every single one of those fruitless attempts to feel cherished by a man. I repeatedly gave myself headaches, thinking about the "bad man" stuff and how it fit with the fact that I seemed to always end up wanting to be alone even after I thought I wanted so badly to belong to someone.

That was a weird state of mind. It felt anything but normal to flip my thoughts from boob loss to failed marriages. However, taking that time to be brutally honest with myself helped me decide what the rest of my life would be.

Also during the waiting period, I was offered a cover story assignment from a magazine in Naples. I thought it would do me good to get out of the house and get my mind on something other than pink ribbons and a flat chest. So I accepted the work.

And guess what the story was about?

God intervened big time.

I found myself sitting at a coffee shop at Coconut Point with a woman who had undergone bilateral mastectomy.

I pay close attention to the messages and movements of the universe. And because I don't believe that anything happens accidentally, I took that chunk of time to mean that I had better get a few pairs of big-girl panties so that when I peed them, I had another pair to wear. Though nothing had been confirmed medically, I knew to my bones that I was headed toward bilateral mastectomy. The tears I shed that evening with that wonderful woman reminded me that she made it and she was amazing. Susie, my friend on Facebook, made it through breast cancer and she was incredible. That meant that I could definitely survive this, too. The difference between those women and me was that I had no husband. However, God has blessed me all of my life with beautiful friendships. Many friends offered to drop everything, come to Florida and see me through this awful time. I was so grateful when they reached out to me. My parents were helping me. When I felt that I was exhausting them, I promised to call on my friends for back-up.

I also found myself grieving the breasts I had not yet lost. I was hyper-sensitive to all the TV commercials featuring busty women in sophisticated evening wear and busty women posing in rather slutty bikinis. I noticed every single breast size on beautiful women. Cringed at the jokes on Facebook about breasts. Teared up about remarks from the other gender, describing themselves as "a boob guy." What would my life be like if I lost my breasts? When those thoughts got too painful, I threw myself into the passion that keeps me moving through anything: words. I tried to find a word that perfectly described how it felt, not just to face breast cancer alone but to look at my future as a single woman without breasts.

The only word that came to me was "empty."

*This post was written in **Nov. 2013**:*

Since that last divorce, I am stuck with a slimy feeling ... that maybe this time, I was broken for good. Thinking about the possibility of losing my breasts ... well that does nothing for the old self-esteem, either.

At this age, most of us don't have a nearly perfect body anymore. But what would it be like to lose my breasts? When I think about that, it is almost too difficult to breathe around the

31

pain and grief.

I have no idea what is ahead. None of us do. We are all like the blind leading the blind. Some of us a lot more damn blind than others.

Maybe someday God will send a truly good man to my life. And maybe He won't. And that is okay too.

Whatever is ahead of me, I have faith that I will get through it. God always shows up.

I must remember that I am more than my failed marriages and more than maybe losing my breasts to cancer. I am more.

November 2013

A few nights ago, one of my dear friends, Tammy, showed up with baked spaghetti and garlic bread, packed so pretty in a picnic basket. Smiling and barely looking in my direction, Tammy stumbled quickly through a greeting and added that yes, she knew I didn't want visitors. But she was worried and had to see for herself that I was okay. She brought food in case I didn't feel like cooking.

I don't remember exactly but I don't think I invited her to stay and visit. I stayed out of hugging range too, because if Tammy reached for me, if she touched my hand ... well I knew that my heart would break open. Even though I knew she wouldn't judge me, I tried to keep a concrete wall between us.

A few nights after Tammy's visit, another friend, Kat, showed up with what she called "a pile of smiles." She brought me colorful, funny, artsy little keepsakes. And I managed to keep myself together until she left.

I was thinking later about the secrets I learned about life while writing my weekly humor column in Indiana.

First, I was stunned by how quickly my column became so popular. And then I started to study the reasons. I discovered that people of all ages, people from all walks of life, love to laugh. They love to be surprised. They love to take a moment away from their concerns and worries, to simply laugh.

Second, I realized that other people appreciate honesty. They related to my words. They seemed to appreciate that I learned a long time ago not to take myself very seriously.

And third, my readers seemed to respect transparency. Through them, I learned that when you have absolutely nothing to hide, other people lovingly accept you. They have plenty of dents and bruises, too.

Simply telling the truth can be hilarious. Laughter and honesty bring people together. So why wouldn't I want to give that away every week in that column?

Of course, by putting myself out there every week in newsprint, I paid some consequences. In fact, I still "pay" for topics I write about on my blog. I still pay for things I say in my books.

There will always be people in the world who want to sink their teeth into your truth and hold it against you. But I nicely remind the nasty ones that that no one forces their eyeballs to focus on my work. Since it upsets them so much, they should avoid it.

But the occasional hits I take for writing about real life never hurt me badly enough to consider gathering all my skeletons and stuffing them back in my closet.

I have a huge box filled with every single letter and card my readers sent to me during those years at the newspaper. I have emails and cards that women have sent to me after they read my books. Some of those letters are stained with tears. I treasure so much that they trusted me with their pain and secrets. That they could feel through my words that I would never judge them.

In that box, I always find more than enough reminders for why I do what I do.

Chapter Five

Today I was thinking about my humor column and my work, in general. Sometimes I still can't believe the blessings I've had in my life. I started writing stories when I was a little girl. I was in love with how my imagination could take me anywhere. If I decided that I wanted to live in a castle, I wrote a story about it. I spent hours and hours writing. One of my elementary school teachers sent a note home, telling my parents that I showed talent with writing. I held onto that little purple piece of paper for years. And I've always been sad that somehow, it got lost from me.

By the time I reached high school, I wrote funny little features for the school newspaper and love stories for my friends about fantasy futures with their boyfriends. At the time, I thought that earning a journalism degree would be the only way for me to write for a living. But in the late 1970s, there were very few female journalists. I was never exposed to magazine writing. I never thought about studying literature and becoming an educated author. I didn't seem to have the skill to look at a bigger world past the one I knew already. So I decided that since I couldn't write as a career, my next love would be working with people with developmental delays.

When I went to college, I declared a major in special education. But I absolutely hated it. My brain is composed of a bunch of ping pong balls. So choosing education as my major was not a good idea. I was painfully bored with the curriculum. I dropped out of college my sophomore year. Then I found myself alone, with a baby on my hip and no education.

It didn't take long for me to see that if I didn't finish my degree, I would never be able to provide for my son. Also, I felt a very strong need to accomplish that goal. When my son was six years old, I went back to college. A few months away from his ninth birthday, my little boy watched his mama tearfully accept her college diploma. And by the way, I switched my major from special education to psychology and went to work in social services. It was the field I was working in when I attended college the first time.

I never fell out of love with writing, though. Late at night and on weekend nights, I wrote books. But the pages were stacked in boxes once I finished them. I went to bed many nights, dreaming that someday I would write one special book that would launch my career.

I was 40 years old when I was surprisingly hired by the Daily Journal newspaper. I say it was a big surprise since I had no background in journalism. Here's the awesome part about that new career move, too: At the interview with the editor, I very strongly felt my Grandma's presence in his office. I left there feeling confident even though I knew absolutely nothing about the business. I was not computer savvy, either. In fact, I only type with one finger since I was booted out of high school typing class for fooling around too much.

Initially, I was in charge of a weekly newspaper for the Greenwood area, which was a slightly larger city maybe twenty minutes north. I spent very long 12- and 14-hour days in that building, trying to teach myself how to do page layout and how to correctly send the finished pages to press. I didn't care how much time it took; I intended to master that job. Very stubbornly, I went to work many mornings before anyone else arrived. I cried out of sheer frustration and was humiliated countless times for the stupid mistakes I made. But I continued to try. My goal was to first get a handle on the computer side of my job. And then, somehow, I would convince the editor to at least give me a chance to write something other than obituaries and the little weekly publication that no one ever read.

On a whim, I started writing a humor column for the weekly newspaper. One day someone called the editor and suggested that he print my humor column in the daily newspaper. The very first column I ever wrote for the Daily Journal was about Bill, Hill and Monica. So that gives you an idea of how long ago that happened. I was so thrilled when readers started to call and laugh and encourage me. More than once, I left my desk after one of those sweet calls and cried in the ladies room, overcome by how thankful and blessed I felt. To be able to write for a living, after all of those years when I wished and prayed so hard for this opportunity, well it was sometimes just unbelievable. And then one day, the editor gave me an actual assignment. Soon after, I was writing full time as a member of the newsroom staff. I was absolutely in love with my work.

With time, I started to see that if I had studied journalism in college, it would have been the wrong decision. I'm not a journalist; I am a writer. There's a big difference between the two. And experience alone was what taught me where I fit best. Our second editor at the newspaper allowed me to push the limits in a fairly conservative community and discuss controversial issues that some readers did not want to hear about. I loved that she trusted my judgment. I loved that I developed a thick enough skin to go ahead and write some stories that definitely put me in hot water with some members of the community. I saw my job as a wonderful avenue for showing all the different faces and lifestyles surrounding county residents, not just the ones they wanted to know about. For example, some readers were angry when I wrote the stories of same-sex families. But that didn't mean those families weren't out there. It didn't mean they shouldn't have a voice. And it certainly didn't mean that I would cower to a few bullies and stop writing about topics they viewed as taboo, either.

As any circle leads from this to that, I realized later that by studying psychology and having training in crisis work, I could handle telling difficult stories through the newspaper —stories about terminally ill children, vehicle fatalities and other painful community losses. I also realized that if I hadn't left the newspaper, I would never have had the time to pursue my dream of writing books.

As far back as I can remember, people always seemed to seek me out when they were hurting.

I take it very seriously when others trust me with their deepest hurts. I believe that every time life wounds you in some way, it makes you sparkle with new wisdom. And the more you sparkle, the more frequently others share their pain with you.

I've learned a lot by listening to people talk about their disappointments and struggles. We all have dealt with some level of hurt in our lifetime, of course. But some of us seem to get more than our fair share of loss and pain. Through my work, I met amazing people who faced circumstances the rest of us probably could never fathom, much less survive. So I know that when you stop hiding pain, wonderful things happen. When you encourage the secrets to leave your mind and stop defining who you are, you set yourself free.

A long time ago, I started to imagine my soul as a transparent, flimsy piece of fabric, fluttering in the wind. Now that I am in my fifties, I know much more deeply that when we stop hiding from our failures and heartaches, weaknesses and fears, the breezes of life drift right through that fabric of the soul.

I am so thankful to know that only a transparent soul will dance in the breeze.

Chapter Six

During the day, I could occasionally take a break from morbid thoughts. Sometimes I paused the worrying by riding my bike or taking walks and stopping to chat with neighbors. After the sun went down though, breast cancer camped out in the middle of my exhausted cerebellum. I was tempted to repeatedly Google the subject and then send myself into an emotional spin that nearly always resulted in an all-night round with diarrhea. My stomach was nervous and queasy.

My mind was impossible to lasso and keep centered on anything but boob troubles. And then one night, my memory wandered back to the day I wore a training bra for the first time. I smiled, remembering that my friend and I coordinated our clothing choices on that special day. We both wore white blouses so the boys seated behind us in class could see our bra straps when we leaned forward at our desks. I remembered middle school P.E. classes and how embarrassed I was when my new boobs jiggled under that ugly navy blue outfit. By the time I was in high school, my boobs were bigger than a lot of my friends'. I hated how they bounced when I rushed to class. Then I thought about how my breasts swelled with milk while I was pregnant. How amazed I was, to nourish my only child with my body. I thought about the sound of my baby swallowing milk from my breasts. I thought about all the years in the workforce, stuffing my breasts into a minimizer bra, then hiding them even more with too-large blouses, all in an effort to be taken seriously. All in an effort to go to work every day and raise my child without being treated like a sex object. With my 54-year-old eyes, I look back now and feel angry with myself. I shouldn't have bought into the bullshit — that my only safety was to cover everything about me that was female.

No.

Instead of hiding my breasts, I should have mashed a few Neanderthal mouths. I should have kicked a few sets of testicles across the room. That is exactly how I should have handled it. But of course that stuff is easier to think about now than it was then. As a single mother, stressed out by life in general, I was afraid of conflict. I ducked sexual harassment by male co-workers and male clients, too, by hiding my big knockers. My goal was to get through my work days without feeling like some weirdo's wet dream.

Thirty years ago, I commuted to the north side of Indianapolis to work in the mental health field. On weekends, I worked in bars for extra money. Not a good atmosphere, by the way, for a woman who already had a low opinion of the opposite sex. However, the weekend babysitter arrived at my son's bedtime. So working in a bar took less time away from being with my child, and it was fast money. Occasionally I complained about how I was treated in bars. Other people reminded me that I should expect that behavior in a bar atmosphere. But I disagreed; men should be respectful to women, whether they are drunk, sober or just plain stupid. While I bent over to clean tables, I was actually bit on the hind-end a couple of times. Money was stuffed in my bra. Filthy things were whispered in my ear when I thought I was getting a drink order.

By the time I reached my mid-thirties, I grew some backbone. But between the disrespect at the bars and the times I was ripped off by mechanics and bullied at work by male colleagues, I also developed a bad mouth as I grew older ... a bad mouth that could spew like a machine gun. And had a lot of bite to it, too. I could unleash a string of the worst cuss words, sprinkled with sarcasm. I could and would take a man out verbally if he was disrespectful toward me. Instead of wilting when a goofball glued his eyes to my chest, I very often snapped, "Yes they are real, moron," and walked away. I still remember that delicious "Don't fool with me" feeling.

Is that my nature? No. Actually, I hated to step into that other personality. But I had a child to raise in a very difficult, good-old-boy world. I was not willing to back down unless the fight just wasn't worth the win.

Now that I am much older and so much wiser too, I understand that all men aren't the cousins of Satan. I am thankful to personally know a lot of wonderful men who stood by their kids after divorce. Men who never considered cheating on their wives. Men who are as honest as the day is long. I am deeply saddened by the fact that I allowed myself so many years of feeding off my own anger and disappointment. I was unfair to the other gender, very unfair. For too many times to count, I was a fire-breathing dragon, believing that all men were out to get me. I feel sorry now for my porcupine approach. But I'm not a bit sorry for the strength I gained from constantly feeling like a target. And not a bit sorry either, for the ways that I bloomed into a feminist.

Sherri Coner

Chapter Seven

More than a week of waiting and agonizing went by before I learned that my insurance denied payment for BRCA testing. Then I realized that I was no longer depending on the results, anyway. My intuition continued to gnaw at me.

I had to get a mastectomy. Had to do it.

Nov, 8, 2013:

I didn't have three grand stuffed in a cookie jar, waiting to be used on a rainy day or to maybe buy myself some BRCA testing,

So I had to let go of the fact that, at least for now, I will not know whether I carry the gene mutation.

It makes no difference in regard to my decision or the outcome of my treatment, but having that information would be valuable for my son, my nieces, my future granddaughters.

I sat down a bit ago to again study the educational literature.

Every year, I have watched on TV as people gathered to support breast cancer research. And yes, every year I noticed that the sea of pink seemed to swell. I assumed that increase in participants was linked to women and the men who loved them finally getting involved to support a cause.

But here's the reason for that massive crowd of pink-wearing women and those who love them: Current statistics show that one in eight women will be diagnosed with breast cancer in her lifetime.

Unbelievable.

One in eight.

That is a damn epidemic. Where have I been? Why haven't I paid more attention?

I thought about something not-so-nice ... but oh well, I will share it anyway. Ready?

I thought about how different things would be if one in eight men was at risk to develop cancer of the penis, which would, in many cases, lead to amputation of the little soldier.

Well ... male scientists and male doctors would never rest until they secured a way to keep all penis-wearing people intact. They would declare a health emergency. Blah. Blah. Blah.

I entertain myself for a minute with that vision. Then I turn back to the stack of information given to me at the genetic testing appointment.

I barely digested the one in eight statistic before I read the cold hard facts about testing positive for the BRCA gene. The risk of developing breast cancer increases by 87 percent if a woman receives positive results for the gene mutation. Her chance to develop breast cancer a second time rises by 64 percent.

Even though the general population of females has less than 1 percent chance to develop ovarian cancer, testing positive for the BRCA gene shoves a woman's risk to 44 percent.

The faces of my young nieces popped into my head. I closed my eyes and blew my nose.

A few years ago, my doctor suggested the BRCA test. But I was not informed of these incredible statistics. I chose not to do the test. I didn't want to feel like I was constantly living under a cloud if the test was positive.

I wasn't ready to do an Angelina Jolie decision of testing positive for the gene and then rushing in for a mastectomy. I much preferred to live by faith ... a "whatever is supposed to be is exactly what will be. So I don't want to interfere with that. I don't want to make decisions before I absolutely have to make them" approach to life.

Well guess what, Sherri Coner ... "whatever will be" has not only knocked on your door but broken every window in the house.

For a few minutes, I shamed myself for not choosing to get tested more than five years ago. It was yet another one of those, "If I knew then what I know now" moments that leads to absolutely nothing but a heavy heart and a headache from bawling.

Chapter Eight

I have always been high strung. I travel full throttle through life. My mind never shuts off. I never want to miss anything, either. Even if it's bad stuff, it is still an experience. I have always taken pride in my ability to bounce back from a big slap from life. To go through a difficult time but find a way to make fun of it and get right back in the world, rarely missing a beat. To other women, especially single mothers, I explain doing what you are terrified to do in a simple way: "Put your head down and plow." I talk to them about shoving right through the middle of the fear. Dare yourself. Force yourself. But do it. Even when you are filled to the maximum with dread, just go on. Keep moving. Do it anyway.

Breast cancer, however, stole that skill from me. I was bouncing about as well as a concrete block. I couldn't stand noise or hateful people. I absolutely could not stand surprises. I could cry a river at any moment without having one single idea why tears were again streaming down my face.

November 2013:

What a day. It is almost 9 p.m. I am so tired I feel dizzy. Yep. Stress has beat me half to death.

This afternoon, I was scheduled to undergo a second breast MRI. Even though I didn't want to, I started to worry at 7 a.m. What if the MRI reveals cancer in my left breast? What if it's worse than what they found in the right breast?

I did everything I could to stay busy. People who know me know that I am at wit's end when I crank my best music and start to clean house like a wild woman. I hate to clean. It's a big waste of life.

But I did it in an effort to get my mind off the need to buy a cemetery plot before undergoing the MRI.

While I sat in the crowded waiting room, I got a call from the gynecologist's office.

"Sherri, your pap smear shows precancerous cells. We need to see you."

Instead of perking up, asking questions, getting to the core of the call, I returned to the fog. "What? What did you say?"

Inside, I was already thinking, "Does this mean I am on my way out? Do I have cancer all over my body? Oh dammit. I can't breathe."

I started to imagine that little Pac Man character trolling through my body, eating up everything healthy.

I finally got enough sense to ask to speak to the doctor. She wasn't in the office today.

Shit.

When my name was called for the MRI test, that is when I learned that an IV was required, to shoot dye into my veins. Unprepared for this, I started to blink a thousand times a minute, trying not to break out in a big sob festival.

For the test, I must lie flat on my stomach. There's a place on the padded table for my face and a hole for each of my girls to hang down under the table. On another day, I might find this situation to be rather hysterical, much like the day I got the breast biopsies.

But today I am preoccupied by the precancerous cells on my cervix and what I will experience when the dye shoots into my body.

The technician tugs on both breasts like they are cow udders. And again, I bypass all the funny stuff I could see in this moment ... on another day ... when I wasn't worried that I was lying here on this table, dying.

This shit would be crazy funny if I wasn't imagining that I now have ovarian cancer, too.

The technician repeats a couple of times that I must be perfectly still. This is difficult. I have a bad back and it is already beginning to scream. My shoulder joints are killing me because my arms are pulled over my head. I didn't know this was how things would be. Why in the hell isn't anyone preparing me for these moments?

"You can do this," I whisper as I am rolled into the MRI tunnel.

Thankfully, the pap smear results turned out to be nothing except a slight infection. No cancer. But my doctor told me that very likely, she would decide to remove my last ovary. Breast cancer and ovarian cancer apparently like to pal around together in a woman's body. I dreaded that, especially when I did not yet know the course of treatment for the breast cancer. But I also didn't want to worry about developing ovarian cancer.

At night, I scrolled through a couple of different websites devoted to tattooing the flat chests of breast cancer survivors. I decided that definitely, I would have lotuses tatted where my nipples would have been. That idea came from my friend Becky. The lotus pops up from murky, muddy water to bloom on the surface. In many Eastern religions, the lotus symbolizes spiritual enlightenment.

Then my friend Sara shared a quote with me: "May I live like the lotus, at ease in muddy water." Immediately, I fell in love with that quote, wrote it down and taped it to the fridge.

"If anybody knows how to survive in muddy water, it's me," I whispered to myself. "That quote is about me. And I can commit to wear it forever on my chest."

Thinking about creating my own canvas made me feel stronger. Knowing how I would deal with my scars made me feel nearly happy. My tattoo plans would lead to a beautiful and meaningful message on my skin. It would be my plan to cover my pain. The skin art across my scars would be my way of having the last word.

November 2013:

Once again, I was in the oncologist's office.

And once again, my right boob was the star of the show.

"I am so sorry," the doctor said gently as he once again inspected Alex ... as if he hasn't already seen her 47 times in the last 17 days.

"Sherri, did the plastic surgeon say anything to you about this?"

Suddenly, I was holding my breath, hoping he would not announce that, by the way, now they needed to remove half of my belly button ... plus part of my chin and maybe one knee.

"What are you talking about?" I asked cautiously, while trying not to start screaming and crying ... because ... well, by now I cannot take one more thing.

I waited, swallowing hard, feeling my knees start to shake.

"Sherri, we won't be able to save your nipples," he said.

I stared at him, trying to make sure he was serious. I was amazed by this ... but in that moment, I swear I thought I was going to laugh.

Since I am pretty much a whack job at this point ... with no sleep and very inconsistent snot concerts ... I again asked what he was talking about.

He repeated the bad news. And I just passively shrugged.

For heaven's sake, I am losing both of my breasts.

Does the doctor really think I will lose my damn mind over a couple of silly little nipples?

I already assumed I would lose them ... since they happen to be attached to my rotten breasts.

"We can surgically make you some nipples."

"No thanks."

"Well, you can think about it," he said.

"I have thought about it," I said nicely, even though I was now starting to get pissed off.

In my head, I'm thinking, "Do you really believe it comes down to nipples for me? That I will feel totally okay with having my breasts sawed off my body just as long as I can one day look forward to getting a couple of pretend nipples tatted on a couple of skin mounds that won't have any sensation? Is that what you think I'm about?"

I took a deep breath and reminded myself that I am exhausted. It's not nice to be mean and hateful to the nipple-loving doctor. How would he know that I don't give a damn about getting some jacked-up nipples?

I just want to make it through this.

I just want to stop crying. I want to survive the awful fear. I want to live my life again and look forward.

And by the way, I have a whole lot more to look forward to than two fake nipples on two fake boobs.

"I've decided that I am only going through this one time," I said evenly. "That's why I am doing the two-for-one boob removal. And then I am going back to my life. And I don't mind not having nipples to take with me."

Here's the thing ... I am very grateful that I am a candidate for implants. After being big busted all of my life, I think it would be very difficult to go from a double D long to nothing.

A bit of pretend boob is perfectly okay with me, just so my clothes hang a little nicer.

But no nipples? No sweat.

November 2013:

Saw the oncologist again today to get the results of the MRI.

I was up all night, scared to death. I want to hear the results and yet I don't. I want to believe there are no other cancerous surprises. But I am afraid to set myself up. If I hear something bad ... I might not be strong enough to stand up.

But I have to stay strong. I have to keep hope in my front pocket.

Once again, I started to bawl when I got to the exam room. Damn it.

Being given that little white robe makes it too real. And before I realize it, I am cracking up.

I am terrified to hear the results.

God, I can't even breathe. I feel so sick. I practice some deep breathing, to calm myself down.

Thank you, GOD! The MRI showed nothing more than what

was found in the initial mammogram.

I am so mentally drained. I feel like I have been walking against the wind.

But ... no new cancer detected. Thank you, God.

November 2013

Maybe breast cancer would be easier if I were in a longtime relationship. If I had a man who was with me when the girls were perky. A man who was still here beside me when the girls hung their heads toward my waist line. A man who would never think of leaving, even if I lose my breasts.

Trying to say "I have breast cancer" without flinching has put a whole new spin on my life.

So many emotions roll around inside my head, and some of them find a place to knot in the middle of my stomach. There is nothing easy about this.

My faith has carried me through many storms in my life. But this is different.

I ask God for courage and strength. I suppose He is sending more than I realize because sometimes I am standing for longer moments than yesterday or the day before.

Sometimes I feel that I can definitely get through this.

And while I do, I will be looking for what I am supposed to learn from this experience.

November 2013

Today I thought about when people are blamed for not

knowing something that everyone else believes they should have known.

Like a woman oblivious to the fact that her husband molested her child.

Like a preacher who had no idea that his church treasurer was grabbing money every Sunday from the collection plate.

Like a woman who didn't know that cancer was growing in her breast.

I studied photos from September 2013, when I attended a book signing in Mount Dora, and then drove over to Cocoa Beach to visit friends, Becky and Meghan, from Indiana.

They were on vacation for a few days, and I fell in love with Meghan's sweet little twin boys.

But those photographs did not offer one hint to me that anything was wrong.

Six weeks after that visit, I'm told that I have breast cancer.

On day 21, I can humbly admit that breast cancer has taught me about control. That in this life, we are not in charge of anything except maybe what we want to wear for the day. And how we choose to treat other people.

I am reminded that I didn't get to choose when or if I developed breast cancer.

I don't even have enough control to decide when I will lose my breasts.

November 2013

I still can't say "I have breast cancer" without my throat filling up with storm clouds.

But then again, I have always been a very emotional person.

During my years of journalism, I covered some absolutely heart-wrenching stories. I have interviewed many, many people, while tears fell off my face and smudged the words on my notepads.

A few people occasionally made comments about my show of emotion being "unprofessional." But I would have felt disrespectful toward families if I sat there stone-faced while they cried about a tragedy in their lives.

When I imagined myself in their position, pouring my heart out, then noting a stone face scribbling notes ... well, I wouldn't feel that they respected my story. I wouldn't trust that person, either.

Even if I wanted to keep my own feelings in check, there was no way I could avoid crying with those amazing people. I felt their pain. I marveled at their courage and faith. Trying to protect myself from their hurt would have been the ultimate disrespect. That's the way I saw it, anyway.

But in the last 22 days, I have cried more than I can ever remember. It is the first time I have ever cried this much for a pain that wasn't someone else's.

Chapter Nine

Now the mastectomy is scheduled. I am afraid I will lose my mind before the actual date. I try to remember that since this diagnosis, I have learned how to breathe through fear. Waiting on test results has taught me a level of courage that I never knew I had. Knowing that I could be told at any moment that I have lumps and masses and all kinds of you-are-almost-dead problems has definitely changed me. I know now what courage feels like. In my case anyway, courage prickles under my hair. It heats my chest. It gives me a slight chill as a wave of raw emotion washes over me. And the same thought stomps through my head: "I will do anything to live. I will do anything."

Somehow, through all of the stress and crying jags, I have remained upright. I could never say how proud I am of that fact. I might not sleep more than an hour at a time, but I am still moving. Still taking steps, even if I have no idea where in the hell I am headed.

I have no idea how to cope with the mastectomy. It is a dread, building up in the middle of my gut. It is a burning, breathing monster that crushes my lungs when I try to take in a full breath. I don't know how to lose my breasts. I don't know how to prepare for this change in my life. Other breast cancer survivors would be happy to talk to me about this. They would be willing to listen to me talk. But I can't talk about it. I can only sob my damn head off. I am worn out and scared to death. I am exhausted from trying to act like I am okay. But I am so very far away from okay. I just hope I can keep my soggy brain from falling out of my head. In a matter of days, I will be mutilated forever. It is difficult to shove that realization out of the way and make room for "But you will be cancer-free. So who cares about your boobs being chopped off your body?"

I care.

I care a lot more about having breasts than I ever knew. And now, the countdown has begun. I will be losing a couple of pieces of my womanhood. I feel shallow and scold myself for grieving my breasts. But I do it anyway. I grieve for the way my body will change. The way my life will change.

I fall asleep on the couch and wake up with my heart in my throat after a nightmare involving a Samurai sword in the operating room.

Nov. 29, 2013

Missed the trash truck. Dang it. So I am just leaving the trash can by the road.

After my surgery on Monday, I will spend only one night in the hospital. I will go to my parents' condo on Tuesday. As soon as I am strong enough, I will come home.

I don't know what to expect in regard to recovery. I am usually able to overcome, though.

For example, I was back to work five days after a partial hysterectomy.

Twenty years later, surgery on the joints of both feet hit me a lot harder. Last year's surgery on my neck wasn't a picnic, either.

Maybe my Super Chick cape is a lot more wrinkled than I like to admit. For all I know, it's got a bunch of holes in it. And that can't be good, either.

As Monday gets closer, the knot in my stomach gets bigger. I have no appetite, but I make myself eat. I don't want to go in there, weak and rundown.

I can't sleep. I have not slept more than a couple of hours at a time in 24 days.

I am fixin' to see fear ... I imagine it will be tangible. I can maybe reach out and touch it.

I imagine that fear looks like heavy cloaks, woven together by big, dark snakes. I am afraid I will suffocate if I don't get a grip.

I have been afraid plenty of times in my life. But this is different. This is a deep terror and it is impossible to run away from it.

On Monday, I will be changed forever. And I will never, ever have my own breasts again.

I am so very thankful to be alone until the surgery. My stomach is a wreck. But at least I don't have to worry about upsetting anyone else with my very ugly moments.

The odd thing, though ... the odd, comforting thing is that I know I am supposed to go through this. I know I am supposed to share it on my blog. Every bit of it ... no holding back.

It takes guts to be authentic and transparent. But I am those things. Even when I am bawling my eyes out, I am still those pieces of courage. And that gives me pride.

Every time women write to me, I know all over again why I have breast cancer.

I love that God trusts me with such an important responsibility.

On Monday, I will find the courage to cope with my fear.

59

I will do everything I am supposed to do because this is what God expects of me.

I might be hard-headed. And yes, I can be a smartass, too. But I have enough sense not to ever question God and His plans.

Chapter Ten

Thanksgiving Day came and went with the usual sting that every divorced person in the universe understands. But I barely paid attention. I was trying not to be squashed by that big "your mastectomy is Monday" monster. It was relentless. I didn't know if I could hold up under the fear. Maybe to avoid thoughts about my soon-to-be-boobless chest, I returned to a topic that had absolutely nothing to do with my breasts.

Once again, I buried myself in introspection about my disastrous history with men.

Instead of my usual "poor me, my men always break my heart," approach, I finally worked up the nerve to ask myself what was wrong with me. What was it about me that brought hurtful situations into my life. What was it? What broken places did I have? Where exactly were they located? My heart? Soul? Psyche? Where? How broken were those pieces? And could they ever be healed?

I thought about patterns. Lord knows I have definitely lived a pattern. I only attract emotionally crippled men — some with drinking problems, others with an addiction to sneaking, cheating, lying. Believe me, narcissists love me, too. It was an ugly picture. But then again, the truth is always the hardest to see. In a nutshell, I spent my heart on men who happily gobbled up my kindness, then used it against me as a weakness.

I never knew when I would reach my limit. But in my mind, I started to pack an imaginary suitcase. Every time I was lied to, taken for granted and purposely hurt, I mentally packed another piece of who I was. I never knew when the suitcase would snap

61

shut. But when it did, I was out the door. I left all three marriages — never looked back, never even considered trying to work it out. Just shut the door and locked it.

What did that behavior say about me? Maybe I was the one with the commitment phobia. Maybe I was the one who couldn't be emotionally available.

After all, it was me who ran away instead of trying harder. Maybe I purposefully made bad choices in mates so I could disengage faster and with far less emotional pain. Or maybe one or two of those husbands would have been more nurturing had I not constantly presented myself like I was a wall of steel.

During all of that deep thinking, I realized a couple of truths. One, that I lied to myself every single time I laughed and told people that I was low maintenance. That all I needed from a man was some occasional sex and the ability to kill mice and change storm windows. That's not true at all. I was just so full of shit for so many years. More than anything, I needed a husband who would wrap his arms around me, tell me constantly that I was cherished and mean it from his soul.

To admit that to myself made my cheeks burn. Immediately, I felt weak and girly. But the truth was the truth. I did need that. I had always needed it. And I still do. I just wasn't willing to ever admit it, much less ask for it.

Second, I realized that I should have learned how to allow a man to take care of me. I should have stopped being such a bad ass all the time. I should have learned how it might feel to be protected by someone. But it terrified me to feel that vulnerable. I never felt safe about letting my guard down. Never felt that a man had eyes for only me. That he would fight off any kind of monster for me, either. I viewed myself as dispensable. And apparently, that is also how I viewed my men. I entered relationships with one foot out the door, secretly expecting the bottom to fall out of the bucket. I suppose that was self-fulfilling prophecy at its finest. Because always, the bottom fell out of the proverbial bucket, just as I predicted.

Wow. It hurt like hell to dissect myself that way. It was heartbreaking to parade my bad mistakes through my mind. I have spent all of my adulthood working my hind end off and always, always, always connecting with members of the other gender who never once gave back even half of what I gave. I was never married to men who took responsibility for car maintenance or home repairs. The world revolved around their gigantic egos. When dating, I never paid attention to the red flags, such as how much a man drank. But if I did notice that their alcohol intake seemed to be over the top, I immediately made an excuse for it anyway.

When one husband admitted to me that he cheated on his ex-wife, I didn't see that he would more than likely repeat that behavior with me (which, by the way, he did). I didn't pay attention to how the men handled money. I didn't ask questions about their values and goals. I never one time told myself that I deserved more than the crumbs I was occasionally tossed.

Why did I set myself up that way? Well, a yearning to feel loved and safe and accepted was the reason I didn't apply one single ounce of common sense to those relationships. One minute, I wanted to burn my bra and sing "I Am Woman." A few minutes later, all I wanted in the world was to sleep beside someone every night and feel like I belonged somewhere.

I know many women who behave the same way I do. We allow that hole in our hearts to turn us into complete dumbasses. We ignore the negative attributes of our men, hoping we can love them back to being good people, hoping we can fix them. That's how we get left behind with nothing. That's how we end up raising our children with no fathers. When a man has too many character defects to be a decent husband, Lord knows he won't be winning a "father of the year" award, either.

Finally I had the courage to be painfully honest with myself about my very embarrassing past. Breast cancer apparently removed my need to bullshit myself for fifty years. I had to admit to myself that I never had the skills to be in a healthy relationship. I attracted people who were broken, since I was broken, too. During those long, sleepless nights before the surgery, I cried so many tears, wishing that I could have somehow healed myself twenty years ago. Wishing that I had believed in myself, that I had known how to take good care of my heart. That I had viewed myself as worthy. That I had applied some damn common sense to my decisions instead of allowing that desperate, broken feeling in my chest to lead me right on over the edge of self-destruction.

Some serious boo-hooing went on. But none of it changed the fact that on Monday, I would face breast cancer without a life partner.

Nov. 30, 2013:

The moment I opened my eyes this morning, my first thought was, "The day after tomorrow, I lose my breasts."

I have craved quiet today, not wanting to answer the phone, and cussing my guts out when some people repeatedly called back. I know they mean well. But I can't take it.

"Please," I whispered as I turned the volume off on my phone. "Please just leave me alone."

For the last few days, I have noticed the sidewalks getting more crowded. It's snowbird season at the beach. And they are starting to flock, which pisses me off.

Yesterday, some of the bike riders refused to get off the sidewalk when I was walking. So I very politely stepped over in the grass.

But not today.

When the brats on bikes tried today to take over the sidewalk, I refused to budge.

Nope, they can get in the damn grass. They can eat gravel, too.

It felt kinda good to be a mega bitch today.

Maybe tomorrow I will wear a friggin' tiara, decorate my face with war paint and scream at the top of my lungs like I'm psychotic. And the snowbirds will practically fly out of my way on their fancy bikes.

I am pissed off and exhausted and so sad that I can barely hold my head up.

And Monday just keeps on coming. Damn it.

Dec. 1, 2013

Yesterday I was a shrew.

Today I am a monk with an involuntary crying reflex.

I'm getting my things together for post-surgery days, my books, my laptop, my secret things to carry in my purse for good luck.

The nurse advised that for a few days, I would not be able to raise my arms. And it's not good to realize that I have only two button-down shirts to my name. That's okay, though. If I need another shirt, I will borrow one from my dad.

Been trying all day to identify all the emotions that run through my veins.

I wish I had asked my friend Gail to photograph Tiff and Alex before they leave me tomorrow.

I also wish I tried harder to find something to prevent the drainage tubes from dangling. It will be a zillion times more uncomfortable for those awful things to hang loose.

I think of my sweet friend, Theresa, who invented these awesome net bags so the tubes could be stuffed in those instead of dangling while women showered. But Theresa is gone now. Dead from cancer. And I have talked to her spirit more than a few times since she died.

I miss her so much.

It's difficult to think straight and take care of all the responsibilities when you look and feel like the walking dead. My head is full of fog. I am surprised I have enough sense to open the closet door.

For the rest of this day and this night, I am just asking God to please send me some peace and calm.

I also hope for drugs ... heavy-duty, kick-your-ass drugs. Because right now, I cannot bear the thought of seeing the inside of that operating room. I can't breathe when I think about being assisted from the gurney to the operating table.

Right now I do not want to feel that last moment, when I can raise my hands to my chest and know that my breasts are still mine, right there where God put them.

Maybe tomorrow I will feel differently.

But today, I don't think my heart can keep beating through that moment.

Chapter Eleven

When that dreaded morning finally arrived, it was almost a relief. After so many weeks of crying and praying and wishing it would all go away, it was finally D day. The night before, unable to sleep, it suddenly dawned on me that I had prepared nothing. With an eight-hour major surgery ahead of me, anything could happen. It didn't occur to me until after midnight that I might die.

And no one knew what I wanted.

So I wrote letters to my son and daughter-in-law. I wrote a letter to my brother, my parents, friends. I wrote my obituary. I wrote a will, listing who I wanted to have what possessions. Then I put all of these things in a place where I knew my son and daughter-in-law would find them when they came to pack up my stuff. Here's the weird part about that: I didn't do any bawling and squalling. It felt more like a mission. I listed the songs I wanted played at my funeral. I wrote down what I wanted my son to do with my remains. It was an idea I am still in love with ... and that's what I will still ask for one of these days when I have extra money to have a real will drawn up. It was not sad, doom and gloom stuff. It was something to hopefully make my son and daughter-in-law laugh and say something like, "She was always so crazy. Of course she would do something like this on her way out." But ... I won't share it here. It will be a surprise for them when I actually do kick the bucket.

So anyway, the morning of the mastectomy, I first had to see the plastic surgeon. And while I stood topless and perfectly still, she made marks on Tiff and Alex with a permanent purple marker. I cried big, silent tears. They plopped off my chin and drizzled down my chest. She asked me if I was sure I wanted to go through with this and I nodded. I nodded because my voice was drowning. I nodded because I knew that for some weird reason, my intuition had screamed from the beginning that I had to lose both breasts.

Riding in the backseat to the hospital, with my parents in the front, was absolutely hell. They were both stoic. You could see the tension in the air, strangling all of us. They are newly retired in their seventies. They don't need to be all caught up in yet another one of my dramas. I once again decided that the best way to get through this was to go it alone.

We got to the hospital before 11 o'clock in the morning and I went alone to register.

The woman behind the desk read the procedure aloud: "Bilateral mastectomy?" As if I didn't know why I was there. Did she expect me to say, "What? Are you kidding? For heaven's sake, how did this happen? I thought I was here for a tonsillectomy!"

I wanted to punch her square in the mouth. Rude ass. There was no reason to announce to the entire waiting room that I would be leaving my breasts at the hospital. I held my breath, fearing that she would blab about how she lost her favorite aunt to breast cancer. How her friend only had to do lumpectomy. I waited, reminding myself not to knock that mannerless chick into next Sunday.

"Anything else?" I snapped my lips on both of those words. I was shocked when they did not erupt from my mouth with flames shooting off the sides.

Then I disappeared into the restroom. Thank goodness it was not a multiple-stall bathroom. I did not want company. I raised my blouse to investigate the purple marks on my breasts, the dot-to-dot places to cut. I felt nauseous. I pulled my top down again and leaned against the wall, feeling so scared and trapped that I might just finally lose my mind. My hands trembled so badly that I could barely turn on the water faucet. But I did it. And I wet a paper towel, blotted at my sweaty face and tried to calm down. I had no idea how to navigate through the tremendous fear. It was starting to hit me again.

Strangely, it felt like the very first time I heard this news.

This is it.

I have cancer in a milk duct in my right breast.

The surgery is scheduled for today. It will happen today.

Oh my God, when I leave this hospital, I will no longer have breasts.

Somehow I managed to pull myself back together. Stuff my hysteria under my hair. Go back to the area where my parents waited and not say a word about my fear and my sadness and my worries that finally, there is an obstacle in my life that might be bigger than me. I sat on the edge of the chair and felt nearly thankful when my name was called. A few moments later, the nurses gave me a room and started an IV in both of my arms. When my parents entered the room, they pressed their bodies against the sterile white wall and stared at the opposite wall.

My dad's face. My dad's eyes. Well, every time I looked at him, my heart broke.

For weeks, he believed I would breeze right through a lumpectomy. Grab a few rounds of radiation. Jump right back into life before the next commercial break. In his eyes, I saw that he was no longer in denial. His only daughter, his weird, misfit of a daughter, was undergoing a mastectomy today. His eyes didn't even focus.

I didn't want either of my parents to be punished by my pain, so I casually suggested that they go ahead and leave. I didn't tell them why, of course. But I had no idea how I would behave when I was finally rolled down that hallway toward surgery. I wanted to protect them. I already knew that if I started to unravel, it would be loud and ugly. They could not do anything for me. However, I could do something for them: send them away so they did not have to witness my fear.

Many times since the mastectomy, I have thought about the moments between sending my parents to the waiting room and waiting for that final roll down the hallway. And I am still not exactly sure how to describe it. In some ways, it felt like a fast forward of feelings. For a few seconds, I was so terrified that my trembling body shook the entire bed. I started crying so hard that I couldn't breathe. I felt like I was falling into a big, dark pit where real terror would finally destroy me. I started whispering to myself, "It's okay. You will be okay. You are strong. You can do this."

Just when my mind started to whirl around like a tornado and turn into a big, fat crazy spell with a bunch of wailing and howling, the sobbing turned into quiet little sobs dotted with one sentence, over and over. "I know you are with me, God."

That memory of my aunt, sobbing on the gurney, came back to my mind. In this moment, I knew exactly how she felt nearly thirty years ago. I didn't want to be conscious when the nurses came to roll me down that hall. I didn't want to see the operating room where the oncologist would sever my breasts from my body. I couldn't stop myself from imagining that. I wondered what kind of instrument he used. Did he just toss my breasts into a trash bag to be thrown away? Wouldn't it help me to survive this if I could bury my breasts? Maybe give them some kind of ceremony, thanking them for nourishing my baby and occasionally helping me to manipulate my way out of a speeding ticket?

I folded my shaking hands protectively across my chest. Felt my breasts resting against my palms. And whispered a thank you. I have lived long enough now to know that all pain comes with blessings. I decided to be grateful for the moment. Grateful to have a front-row seat to my own courage. In these weeks, I have been allowed to truly see what I am made of. Even though I am crying, I feel pretty bad ass. Breast cancer will steal Tiff and Alex away from me. But not my spirit. Not my faith. Not who I am.

December 2013:

As the nurses walked beside the gurney eight days ago, an incredible calm washed over me. Immediately, I knew that hundreds of hands were folded in prayer at that moment.

Hundreds of hands were holding mine in spirit. I thought about the messages on Facebook and email and all the text messages. People knew I was going to surgery at 1 p.m. today. People I have loved forever and people I have never met took time away from their lives to ask God to look over me.

I started to cry. So very grateful to experience such an amazing moment. So thankful to absolutely know to my soul the power of prayer.

It was an incredible, prayers-are-real reminder. I was literally being carried to that operating room by those prayers.

Mentally, I wrapped that moment in soft pink paper and stuck it inside my heart to keep and cherish forever.

As the nurses transferred me from the gurney to the operating table, I was shaking again. Shaking all over. Trying to clear my head enough to grab hold of something safe. But my fear was fed by the bright lights. Sterile gowns. Utensils gleaming across crisp white paper.

I felt vomit rise in my throat. I have never in my life been frightened enough to throw up.

Pee my pants, maybe. But not to throw up.

71

I thought about the YouTube video I watched, about the woman who danced in the operating room before undergoing a mastectomy. But I didn't feel like dancing. I felt like bolting. I imagined myself jerking the needles out of both arms and jumping off the table to run and run and run to a place where women didn't lose their breasts to cancer.

As the nurse stuffed my long hair into a green paper hat, I thought, "This is it. You have to do this."

But again, just as quickly as that fire-like feeling of terror climbed into my throat, my body was flooded with warmth, with calm. I felt wrapped up in love and comfort. People were praying for me. God was here with me. I could survive this.

As the anesthesiologist placed a mask over my face, I started to worry that God might forget to hang around in here. Desperately, I wanted Him to remember that I needed Him for the next seven or eight hours of surgery. And many more hours after that, too.

I whispered one last time, "Please be with me, God. Stay here with me. Don't leave me in here by myself."

The anesthesiologist sweetly patted my face and I focused on her kind eyes, imagining what the rest of her face might look like under the mask.

"We will take really good care of you, Sherri," She said kindly. "Breathe in. Breathe out. And again ..."

Chapter Twelve

I have fuzzy memories of those first post-surgery hours. But I do remember clearing my head enough to remember where I lost most of a day. I remembered that I had been in surgery. Then I remembered why. I still remember how my stomach dropped as my hands went to my chest. My fingers fluttered across bandages. Big, thick bandages. My torso was encased in what felt like a corset.

God, it was true.

My breasts were actually gone.

When I was released the next day from the hospital, my parents took me to their condo. My dad had moved the living room recliner to the guest bedroom so I could avoid lying flat on my back on the bed. With drainage tubes on both sides of my body, it was impossible to lie on my sides. With fresh incisions on my chest, I could not sleep on my stomach, either.

Before the surgery, I arranged through my insurance for a home health nurse to visit my parents' home. I didn't want my mom to be stressed about helping me with bandage changes. Three times every day, she helped a lot by measuring the amount in the drainage tubes then recording it all for my doctor visits. The nurse, a young woman named Katie, was petite but hugely pregnant and I instantly adored her. Each evening, Katie stopped by to change the bandages. But I wasn't ready to look at my chest. In fact, the bandage changes made me nauseous. Occasionally, the gauze stuck to the drainage and I fought the urge to hurl all over the floor. I sat on the floor in front of a mirrored closet while Katie changed the bandages. But I didn't wear my glasses. And I didn't "look" at what stared back at me.

I don't remember how many days went by before I finally decided, in the middle of the night, that it was time to investigate my chest. In the guest bath, I very gingerly lifted my pajama top, removed the very uncomfortable corset and the bandages, too. My reflection in the bathroom mirror made me lose my breath for a moment. My chest was a railroad track of deep red lines, vertical and horizontal. Because skin expanders had been placed in the cavities where my breasts had been, I had two small, pancake-looking wads of flesh in place of my double D long breasts. My sweet surgeon had already explained that, as the weeks went by, the skin would slowly grow and the expanders would work their magic. One day, there would be enough skin to cover a couple of implants.

What I saw in the mirror made me feel dizzy. I was devastated. I thought my chest looked like a mangled mess, a true mutilation. I closed the toilet lid, sat down and buried my face in my hands. Without making a sound, I cried, cried, cried. Quietly, so that I didn't wake my mother. But also I think there is less sound when the soul is the source of the sobbing.

I was 53 years old. My chest looked like a scene from a bad horror flick. And I had to find a way to live with that. But what mattered most was that I was still in the world. I needed to remember that I was strong enough to walk to the bathroom and have this little "come to Jesus" time with my own heart. While other women with breast cancer were fighting for their lives or losing their lives, I still had mine. Even if I had to do it in a fly-by-the-seat-of-your-britches way, I would discover the skills to survive all of this. I knew that night that I would never again live my life like I had before. But that didn't mean my life was over, just different. I had to somehow introduce my old self to the woman I would become.

December 2013:

I'm not mincing words. So here's the new affliction: constipation.

And the culprit is pain pills.

I could write a country song about the chick who lost her man, her dog and her boobs ... and how the impossible task of pooping was just the last damn straw.

December 2013

In the last 11 days, my plastic surgeon's face has expressed anything but happiness.

Each time she inspects two areas on my incisions, she makes that sour face. Those areas are not healing well. I've been taking a strong antibiotic to prevent infection.

And she has warned me that I might have to go back to surgery.

I've been awake since 3 a.m., anticipating my 8:15 a.m. visit with the plastic surgeon.

"If I am headed back to surgery, I will do my best to hang tough," I whispered to God. "But if you would please place your sweet, healing hands on those two wounds, I would appreciate that so much."

Since I am not yet allowed to drive, my mom took me to the doctor's office. And I immediately started to cough like I had tuberculosis or some other awful affliction.

It was crazy embarrassing, not to mention painful. Maybe someone's perfume bothered me. Maybe I have a new reaction to fear. But all I can say is that fresh incisions on the chest do not mix well with coughing your head off.

I made a beeline for the restroom and dug through my purse to find a five-year-old cough drop or at least a mint. In the mirror, I stared at myself for a moment.

"If you get bad news today, you will rise above," I ordered my reflection. "You are tired. But you will not allow yourself to stretch out and play dead."

I started to cry, stopped and blew my nose.

"This ain't big enough to take you out, Sherri Coner," I hissed at myself. "So you will handle whatever she says. Now get up. And stay up."

December 2013

Today, the doctor wrote a prescription for yet another round of antibiotics and I was so relieved. That meant I had another chance for the wounds to heal.

Since the beginning, I prayed for the awful drainage tubes to simply go away. They incessantly hurt and ached. They peek very sexily under my shirts and blouses. Other people can see this yucky-looking bloody discharge stuff run through the tubing.

I hoped so much that before my birthday, the drainage tubes would finally be removed. Even though I wanted the nasty things yanked out, I was surprised when the surgeon announced that she would remove the tubes. I suddenly froze up with fear. Even though I hated those things erupting from my sides like droopy antennas, I would have agreed to deal with drainage tubes for another year.

I was scared to death. Not ready to deal with a sneak surprise like this one. Not ready at all.

Then I remembered the talk in the bathroom with my chicken-shit self.

I took a deep breath, placed my palms over each side of my chest and tried to mentally prepare for whatever this experience would be. As the doctor pulled the tubing out of my body, I actually felt it uncoil like a garden hose, under my palms. I couldn't decide whether to be mesmerized or sick. It wasn't exactly an unbearable pain. But it wasn't a party, either.

The perk, I hoped, was that once the drainage tubes were removed, I could finally get in the shower.

But no, with the incision troubles, it was not okay yet for me to shower. I had not washed my hair since Dec. 2, the morning of the mastectomy. And so, even though I didn't get that perk, I quickly realized that since I no longer had to deal with the drainage tubes, maybe I could finally rest.

Maybe I could sleep on my side.

Tears filled my eyes as I realized how very badly I simply needed to sleep. If I could just sleep, I could convince myself that yes, here was something from my old pre-breast cancer life that I could have back.

It was like the breast cancer fairies whispered, "Here you go, Sherri. Your consolation prize is rest. Just have some sleep."

December 2013:

Since the surgery 12 days ago, I kinda look at my chest like it's the front of a vehicle ... a car without headlights.

For the life of me, I don't understand how two empty sockets can sting and ache all night. But at least the surgery is behind me.

I got to spend the night at home last night. But because I don't have access to a home care nurse here, I will have to go back to my parents' condo tomorrow. I hated to go to bed. I felt like I was wasting precious time of just being around all my own things again.

I can hardly see to type this ... and thank God no one is here to witness my latest crack-up session. A few minutes ago, I opened my underwear drawer and found my pretty gray bra. I bought it awhile back on clearance. But I have never worn it.

I tossed the new bra on my bed. But then reality and anguish crashed into my heart, all in the same moment.

Down the side of the bed I went, wailing and sobbing like I just now realized that I have no breasts.

For some reason, I still find these jagged edges ... but I don't realize it until I am already bleeding out.

I will never wear that pretty gray bra.

I lost my breasts.

It's true. I lost them. And they will never be mine again.

December 2013

It is raining! What a nice surprise! I love rain so much.

I miss the baby beach house, with rain beating down on the metal roof.

I spend time on the lanai at my parents' condo, watching the rain on the river.

I dance around a little bit. But not much since I feel like I am half mummy. The bandages rub and irritate the skin on my back and sides ... and piss me off.

This quiet Sunday took a definite turn ... directly toward Shit Town.

I noticed that my gown and the bandages, too, were wet on the left side.

Both drainage tubes were removed just last week. But definitely, stuff is leaking from the left drainage site.

One of the nurses warned me that at least one tube might have to be re-inserted.

Oh my God, my eyes fill with tears when I remembered her saying that.

Dammit.

If I wasn't trying so hard to be the positive chick who lost her breasts, I would very likely throw myself a big, messy hissy fit right about now.

On the phone a bit ago, one of my friends reminded me that it's only been two weeks since major surgery. And look how well I'm doing.

I very gingerly add gauze to the still-healing puncture wound of the drainage site.

I decide to focus on all the things that are going right.

I can sit up longer. I can walk farther. I am trying to eat better.

I still need to work on coping skills for surprise pain. When the nerves try to reconnect, I feel like someone shot me or stabbed me or held a torch to my chest.

But I am doing better at breathing through those moments.

I don't want to turn into a mastectomy monster.

I just need to focus.

And remind myself, "You got this. You can do this."

Chapter Thirteen

Like so many other moments that float in my head with no timeline, I cannot recall when I woke from a nap to find an amazing message on my cell phone. The message was from my oncologist, saying that pathology results from my mastectomy revealed lobular cancer, an entirely different type of cancer, forming in my left breast. He commended me. Yes, he saw that I was absolutely correct when I insisted on a mastectomy. Even when I could have chosen the less intrusive option, lumpectomy and radiation, I still said, "Take them off. I know I have to do this."

Each time I listened to the voice message, I felt so grateful. Now the oncologist knew that he wasn't messing around with a wingnut. His voice sounded surprised and a little bit humbled.

Thank you, God, for constantly talking to me, constantly insisting that I opt for mastectomy, no matter how terrified I felt about it. "My intuition is a bad ass," I whispered to myself. "That chick has got her act together."

For many years, I felt but ignored my intuition. And every single time I did that, Life bit me on the hind end. Very often, a warning gurgled around in my gut. But I was arrogant. I chose not to pay attention. Big, painful consequences followed that really bad decision to pretend that my intuition wasn't screaming at me to stop and think or turn in the opposite direction. Life experiences showed me that I should respect that odd little something that prodded and poked at me.

I should acknowledge and trust that my intuition was a wise old lady who knew that I was very often dumber than a door knob.

Intuition saved me from insanity in a couple of bad marriages.

81

It was Intuition that sent me out at night, to look under the seat of an unnamed-ex husband's vehicle. Another time, even though I was called paranoid for suspecting yet another old slime bucket of cheating, Intuition drove me to buy a wig, borrow cars, follow the lying sack of shit and see for myself. Intuition also revealed to me that my "friend" was messing around with my old slime bucket.

I wasn't exactly devastated about the husband's behavior. I sort of expected it, really. But there's a historic rule among girlfriends, you know. Whether I wanted his lying ass or not, my friend was not supposed to sneak around with my old slime bucket. That was the first and hopefully the last time that I ever have to feel that deep cut across my heart. I had never been betrayed by a friend until that one did some hanky-panky with the slime bucket. All these years later, I still smile and envision myself going after her on Jerry Springer.

I imagine my intuition as a very classy wisp of a woman who wears stars and sparkles on her long gown. Her hair is snow white, curled into a no-nonsense bun on top of her head. She sleeps in the moon, unless she is once again trying to steer me away from disaster. She adores me. She wants the best for me. She never judges or leaves me. But she admits often that I test her nerves. I give her headaches.

Through the years, my intuition has definitely rolled her eyes at me. Sometimes she shakes her head and whispers, "When in the world will you stop being so naive?" Yes, she expects me to stand up and find the truth. In the middle of a crisis, my intuition expects me to be brave and strong. If I listened to her more often in the last 50 years, I probably wouldn't have needed a divorce lawyer on speed dial.

No doubt about it, Intuition saved me once again. This time it involved breast cancer, not men. Had I ignored her voice in the beginning of this story, I have no doubt that I would have gone with the lumpectomy. A few months later, I would be right back in the surgeon's office, dealing with cancer in the left breast. Intuition is a sweet mix of God and angel. Over the years I have grown to protect mine and to listen intently when she speaks. Today I am so grateful. Intuition may have even saved my life.

December 2013:

In a few days, I will be 54 years old.

Some women I know freak out about aging. But not me. I happen to love all the goofy lines and ridges on my face. They are old road maps, reminding me of all the places I have traveled to get to where I am right now in this moment.

There are quite a few dead ends on my face ... roads that I either took on my own or was forced by life to take. There are deep crevices where tears still dribble. There are plenty of laugh lines, reminding me that I know some of the funniest girls in the universe.

I am crazy lucky to be surrounded by some really wonderful people who love me, no matter what.

Getting older brings all kinds of gifts, you know.

I am developing much better skills and abilities, to see through lies, to accept disappointment, to hold on tighter to joy.

For a few years now, I've taken little journeys in my head and floated around in the idea of one day being a sweet little soul's grandmother. For all these years, I dreamed about comforting my child's child against my huge bosom, where he or she could just settle in happily against my flesh pillow.

I never dreamed, of course, that I would be a granny without my breasts. But then again, that doesn't mean I will be less of a granny or less of a woman. I just won't be exactly what I dreamed that I would.

As I age, I learn to trust my heart and, of course, my intuition. I learn that every day, I get closer to the end of my days.

I want to make them count.

I want to move forward in my life, surrounded by all things yellow and bubbly and happy.

I am so blessed that breast cancer, for me, won't lead to the end of my stay on the planet. In this moment, I truly believe I'll continue living for a long time.

I will choose all things that take my breath and make me laugh till I cry. That's what I choose.

Chapter Fourteen

Fifteen days after the mastectomy, just when I was beginning to feel stronger, I returned to surgery. It was Dec. 17, 2013, four days before my 54th birthday. Those two stubborn areas on the incisions had not healed.

I held it together until I changed into that dreaded gown, with the opening in the front. I cried and cried and cried some more, even though I knew why this had to happen. I knew exactly what would be done during the procedure. I also knew that I would leave surgery with new incisions. I knew there was a good chance that I would also have to deal with drainage tubes again. I felt like a baby but I still did the bawling and squalling. To tell you the truth, I just couldn't help it.

God, I was tired.

I was so tired of feeling weak and I was tired of how much it hurt just to climb out of bed. I felt guilty that I couldn't drive, which meant my mom was still in Florida, transporting me to and from my doctor appointments. I felt bad that she and my dad had delayed their winter plans because of me.

"This time it won't be nearly as difficult." My nurse named Ann smiled at me as she started the IV. "But I'm sure you're tired of all this stuff."

I could only nod. I couldn't find my voice because it was buried again by the usual tears and fears and disappointment. The tears slipped off the sides of my face and puddled in my ears. I woke up with a new drainage tube on the left side and new incisions, too.

More and more, I was preoccupied by the limits set by breast cancer. I missed who I used to be. But I did not yet know that I would never be who I once was. That chick was long gone. She might have left when I was doing all that sobbing on the floor before surgery. Maybe she left the moment I placed my hands on my chest and felt only bandages after the surgery. Who knows exactly when she drifted away. But one thing would later be evident. And that was very clearly the fact that breast cancer had changed me forever.

My tolerance for negativity dropped to a cold zero. And I would never again be as much of an airhead. I grew up a lot after the third divorce. I finished growing into my age through breast cancer. And I would never again put up with people treating me badly. I would no longer have patience for any life experience that took any amount of joy away from me, either.

I now knew that I was not safe from experiencing a medical challenge that had the potential to take my life as easily as it took my breasts. Because I learned this, I realized how much of life I have missed. I realized how much I wanted to be here in the world. Of course, we all know that we won't be getting out of here alive. But maybe we don't stop to think enough about what we want to cram into our lives before we lose them. Breast cancer made me feel vulnerable. It replaced my arrogant, I-can-do-anything attitude with a humble sniffle to God that consisted of just a few words: "Thank you for letting me stay here longer."

Chapter Fifteen

Well the second surgery knocked me flat on my hind end for a few days. I hardly knew what day it was. My 54th birthday came on Dec. 21, but I barely noticed. I was so sore. It took my breath to sit up. My poor dad had to gently pull me to my feet. A few times, he slipped my feet into shoes. And even though I appreciated his kindness and my mom's too, I was embarrassed about being and feeling like an invalid. Physically, the second surgery sucked all of my new-found energy. I was back to feeling as weak as I felt after the mastectomy. It made me so mad I couldn't see straight. God knows I will never win an award for patience.

As those late December days drifted by, I cried at night, wishing I had gifts to send to my son and daughter-in-law. I wished to see them, hug them close to me. But I didn't want them to see me in the shape I was in, slowly tottering around and worn out and quickly growing dreadlocks since I still wasn't allowed to get in the damn shower and wash my hair.

By Christmas Day, I felt stronger. I could sit up longer. And I saw that very slowly, I was grabbing hold again of my life. That's also the day I started working with my dad to write his life story. It was a project I had wanted to do for him for a long time. Plus, it took my mind off the fact that it was Christmas but I had no gifts for anyone. I had not sent a single card to anyone, either. I started to view breast cancer as the big black event in my life that stole away so much more than my boobs. But I really enjoyed writing about my dad's life. Beginning with the story of his dad, my grandpa, who went to work as a farm hand at 11 years of age, to support his widowed mother. I saw a lot more sides of my dad that

I never knew. He is truly a self-made man. And I have always been very, very proud of both of my parents for all that they have worked so hard to achieve in their lives.

The day after Christmas, I packed my stuff and announced that I needed to go home. And I mean I really *needed* to go home. I was tired of disrupting my parents' lives. I was tired of being the patient. I was tired of everything related to my flat, bandaged chest. I hated that my mom still had to drive me to all the doctor appointments. But I knew that if I went home, she could at least rest better. I knew she was exhausted.

My dad was not a bit happy with that announcement. He was afraid of infection. He was afraid that if there was an emergency, an ambulance couldn't get across the bridge due to all the snowbirds crowding every square inch of my beloved little five miles of island. I tried to reassure him. But he didn't want to change his mind. And that was one of the first times I noticed that breast cancer has changed me. The "old" me would have gone right back to that guest room, unpacked and agreed to stay so my dad wouldn't be worried to death. But the new chick with the flat chest had to do what was best for her ... meaning me. And what was best for me? I wanted to go home. Finally, I was beginning to handle myself more like a grown woman and less like somebody's little girl who couldn't fend for herself.

Now, wanting to go home and arranging life around my boobless chest were two very different goals. Because I could not bend over or reach above my head, everything I needed had to crowd the kitchen counter of my very small abode. It drove me slightly bonkers to see everything on the counter. Everything in the fridge had to be on the top shelf so I could avoid bending over. Simply moving around was still a problem. My chest was sore. The skin expanders ached all the time. And the ports, located at the bottom of my ribcage on both sides, sometimes slipped in between my ribs. That hurt so badly that it took my breath. I still wasn't sleeping well, either.

Honestly, it was hell to go home and fend for myself.

But it was time.

I was unbelievably happy and thankful that 24 days post-mastectomy and a second surgery too, I was back at the beach. I was again surrounded by all the things I love best. Pictures of my sweet son and my adorable daughter-in-law. Favorite books. Quiet.

I wasn't fantasizing that as soon as I got home, I would miraculously run marathons. I knew it would be difficult. And it was. It was very hard to do. Simple things you don't think about, such as pushing the knob on the toaster or using a manual can opener, opening a jar or tearing off a piece of Saran wrap, flushing the toilet ... those actions were painful. I had no idea there were so many weird muscles attached to my chest until I went through bilateral mastectomy.

But I did not care how difficult some moments were. I believed that if I could be at home alone, in a place I love so dearly, I could heal faster.

Many women tromped in and out of my door. Neighbors stopped by to help with bandage changes. They took my trash to the road for me. They watered my plants. They brought food to my door. Friends stopped by to check on me. Even the sweet mail lady took the time to bring my mail to the porch so I didn't have to walk to the mailbox. All of those gestures from neighbors and friends, coupled with the cards and care packages from so many friends up north and even people I have never met, all of those moments brought me to tears. I was so grateful to be included on so many loving hearts. I learned that lots of people love me, and I cherish that. I learned that lots of people included me in their prayers and cheered me on. I know, to the bottom of my heart, that all of those heart-felt gestures helped me work toward healing, physically, emotionally and spiritually, too.

December 2013

The damn drainage tube on my left side is killing me. As in constantly. It hurts much worse that the drains I had after the first surgery. This constant pulling, throbbing sensation is making me so nervous, I could jump right out of my skin.

My parents drove me to the appointment with the plastic surgeon.

Since I already knew the tube would likely be removed during this visit, I was half sick with anxiety.

I don't invite either of my parents to accompany me to the exam room.

As much as I sometimes wish I had someone to hold my hand in there, I will not be selfish like that. They won't be invited to observe the torture.

I sit on the exam table, once again dressed in a stark white paper vest, I prepare myself for agony.

When the tube is removed, the pain is overwhelming. I feel sick and dizzy.

Twice, the nurse asked if I was alright.

Both times, I lied and said that I was okay. But what I really wanted was a morphine drip and a bed.

By the time I made it back down the hallway to the elevator, I could not keep myself in check any longer.

I broke down in the elevator.

I did exactly what I promised myself I would not do. Right in front of my parents, I lost my damn mind.

I swear I couldn't help it. I just sobbed, uncontrollably.

My left side hurt and stung, first from the doctor digging into the site to get hold of the tube. And then, of course, from the actual unmedicated removal of the tube.

It hurt a zillion times worse than the first time tubes were removed.

My dad drove to the store next-door and my mom went inside to buy a drink so I could take my pain meds.

My dad turns to look at me -- his half-dead daughter -- in the backseat and says, "Did that hurt, Sissy?"

Well it was out of my mouth ... it flew right out of my mouth ... before I could even think to grab hold of those words ...

My response sounded a lot like, "It hurt like a mother heifer."

I won't write what I said since both of my parents are traumatized by my bad mouth.

They don't understand that my cuss-crazy mouth has no connection with them. They fear that other people will look down on them because their 54-year-old daughter has an awful mouth.

But of course, there's absolutely no truth to that.

I'm grown.

I have lived a completely different life than they have. The fact that I'm a potty mouth, well, that's obviously not their fault and doesn't need to be their concern, either.

But anyway ... there it was, the queen of bad words ... flying out of my mouth and smashing all over the windshield of the car.

I believe my dad would have tried to ground me if he thought he could get away with it. He commented that a lady doesn't use such language. And I assured him that I don't ever describe myself as a lady, anyway.

I might be a lot of things ... but I'm not a bullshitter.

What you see or hear is exactly what I am ... and "lady" is not likely to be used as an adjective to describe me ... especially with a straight face. But I am perfectly okay with that.

That day, I reached my limit. I had absolutely had all I could take.

All I wanted was to be alone with my frayed nerves and my throbbing left side.

Since then, I have talked with many other breast cancer survivors who also went to the dark side with language, in moments they could not control.

Only I don't have the excuse of breast cancer like they did ... my mouth is bad, even on a great day.

December 2013

I wrote a tearful thank-you letter to my sweet nurse, Katie. I am very sure that I will remember and love her forever.

Sometimes I feel injured and bruised up.

Sometimes I feel a little bit cheated out of the life I thought I was grabbing hold of, until breast cancer moved that life to an entirely different continent.

This morning, alone now at home, I will don my plastic gloves, remove the bandages and take care of the incisions. I am strong enough now, woman enough now, to accept my scarred chest and all of its care.

I want to be proud of myself. I want to feel like I carried myself through the rest of this trip through all things pink.

I want to carry myself instead of depending on someone else to take care of me. But the other truth to that goal is that I don't really know how to allow other people to take care of me, anyway.

Chapter Sixteen

For many years, my favorite holiday was New Year's Eve.

Sometimes, I got a new dress and made a plan with other single mommies. For that one night, we danced until we dripped with sweat. We laughed until we cried. We stepped out of the role that scared us to death: the job of raising our children alone, raising children who would hopefully grow into strong, loving, kind and successful adults, despite the painful losses in their lives.

I absolutely adored New Year's Eve. I was in love with those last moments of the year before and happily watched old mistakes and disappointments climb into the past and drift away. I was equally in love with the first magical moments of the New Year. I could dream and hope and imagine that this would be the year I finally got it right.

Last New Year's Eve, which was my first in Florida, was spent alone, with a dream that the New Year would unfold with lots of new adventures and opportunities. I put long, long hours into writing and editing my books. Seven days a week, I worked on my books, hoping to make a life for myself doing what I love so much.

My second New Year's Eve in Florida brought this flat chest from breast cancer and lots of introspection. Again, I spent the holiday alone. In the rocking chair on my back porch, I stared out at the blackness, breathing in the heavy, humid night air. Faintly, I heard beach lovers laughing in the distance, maybe at parties down the street. I closed my eyes and smiled, remembering when time wrapped me up so sweetly with laughter and music and friends.

At midnight, fireworks exploded by the pier. It was also my only sibling's 50th birthday. I felt bad about that. Like my plans for

Christmas gifts, the plan for my brother's 50th birthday present had also gone by the wayside.

Breast cancer caused a rearrangement of every single plan and every something I believed to be stable in my life.

But I was very blessed. And I knew that.

Breast cancer had not traveled to my lymph nodes.

Chemotherapy was not necessary.

I didn't have to do radiation, either. I was forced to give up my breasts. But I didn't have to give any more time to breast cancer than what it would take now to simply recover from surgery.

I ached to see my son and daughter-in-law, and I cried when I got a "Happy New Year" text from them. That night, I felt a world away from them. I felt a world away from my friends and their laughter. But at the same time, I knew that what I needed on this particular New Year's Eve night was exactly what I had. I needed to be alone. I needed to think.

I still didn't handle difficult moments very well. I still cried too easily about the dumbest things. Sometimes I still had no idea why I was crying. That fact was very embarrassing. I was angered easily. I could not stand to listen to people gripe and complain and gossip.

I wanted to be alone until I found a way to grab hold of my nerve endings. And I wanted to stay alone unless I could be around positive, loving people.

Chapter Seventeen

According to my doctors, the body struggles a lot when a woman loses her breasts. In fact, the body is in shock for a while. A full year is required to recover from bilateral mastectomy. The muscles and nerves freak out, trying to understand that the female chest is changed forever. Add the incision pain. The constantly aching expanders. The ports, moving around in my lower ribs. No sleep. No appetite. Add the amnesia-like feeling from being under anesthetic for several hours during two surgeries in 17 days, and you've got a train wreck named Sherri.

I decided that my baby steps back to life would begin with weaning myself off the big drugs and physically building my strength. I started by making it down the five little porch steps then to the end of the driveway and back.

After a few days, I walked past one house and then two. And back. After those brief walks, I often had to take a pain pill and rest, flat on my back and pissed off. But I knew that it would get easier. As I continued to increase my strength, I started walking on the sidewalk, which is maybe a block from my baby beach house. Even though I wanted so badly to walk to the beach, there were no benches there. And I knew I would helplessly stay on the sand like a beached whale until someone came along to help me get back up. I moved slowly on the sidewalk and took pit stops on the benches.

The walking was very slow because the skin expanders jiggled and hurt like crazy if I tried to pick up the pace. I don't remember now when I finally made it to the beach. But when I did, I stood there and sobbed. I didn't dare sit on the sand since I would much rather be knocked out with a hammer than to experience the pain of trying to get back to my feet. That was okay. The big deal to me was that I made it over there. I might be so weak that my legs were trembling. But hey, I got there.

And that's what counted.

I was also trying to get back to my work. I needed income. I needed to test how long I could sit up without my chest screaming. I needed to know that even if it happened in little slivers at a time, I was claiming life again. And I still had access to my passion, which is to write.

January 2014

I am so thankful to be working again! And I am taking on some new projects that I never would have tackled before.

The old me would have been too afraid of failure.

The new me needs some gentle prodding sometimes, too. But now that my breasts are gone, I think I might have easier access to my bullet-proof shield.

I have to remember sometimes that the universe would not bring these changes my way if there wasn't a reason for them.

January 2014

I am back in the plastic surgeon's office. Is this appointment a little preview of how I will spend these first months of the New Year?

It's weird, I know. But sometimes I still feel shocked.

I still do a double take in the mirror.

I'm still trying to get this change to register in my head. Well, maybe my heart is where I need to register the change.

For the rest of my life, every single Dec. 2 will be Bilateral Mastectomy Day.

In the doctor's office, I ask again about the skin expanders. Again, she calmly explains that as new skin grows, the expanders will slowly stretch the skin. After a few months, there will be enough space on both sides of my chest for the implants to be surgically placed.

The doctor says it is perfectly normal for the skin expanders to hurt and ache. It is perfectly normal for my chest to sometimes feel so tight that it might pop open. It is normal for the ports to ache and burn from their homes under my skin, on the bottom of my rib cage.

Hmm.

Apparently, it is perfectly normal to feel like death warmed over.

Treatment for the still-healing incisions increases to changing the bandages three times daily.

Each time I change the dressing, I must first soak the gauze in saline.

And here's the fun part: I then place the moistened gauze directly inside the open wounds on both sides of my chest.

That means that every time I change the dressing, I will very carefully pull the gauze away from those extremely tender areas. The gooky discharge stuff will be pulled away from the incisions, which will be anything but pleasant.

To tolerate the bandage changes, I have to go back on stronger pain medication.

I leave the office feeling a little bit afraid of doing these dressing changes alone.

And I leave there disappointed. I still can't take a shower.

But the bright side is that I can drive again!

This news takes pressure off my mom. She can go home to Indiana.

I feel that I am on my way back to my life.

January 2014

I am fighting with anxiety. I can't sleep in my bed. I literally cannot get my breath in there. So I am still sleeping on the couch.

For some reason, I feel safer in the living room, with the TV on all night.

I wish for a sedative and a pacifier. I am sick of it ...

January 2014

The doctor says it is perfectly normal, but I have absolutely no energy.

I have to try harder to deal with this mix of hurt and fear and anger. I have to try harder to find a place to put this overwhelming and unexplainable sadness.

For heaven's sake, I am still here. That should be the only thing that matters to me. That should at least be the first priority.

Most days, it absolutely is the priority. I am here. Thank you, God.

But on other days, I still mourn who I used to be and how I viewed myself.

I still grieve to have back the eyes I had before cancer. Those eyes saw the world in such a different way. Those eyes believed I was absolutely untouchable.

But these eyes see this chest every day in the mirror.

These eyes know that I will never be the woman I was before Nov. 5, 2013, when the doctor called with those four words.

I've heard four words before that hurt me. Words like, "You are so stupid," "I'm done with you," and "I don't love you."

But "You have breast cancer" -- those are the four words that changed me forever.

Chapter Eighteen

To give myself new energy for the second leg of breast cancer treatment, I knew that I had to find something funny about my mess. But that seemed impossible. I was still doing lots of bawling. I was still exhausted from lack of sleep. Those skin expanders and ports made me say cuss words I didn't even know I knew. That was a big shocker since I am an expert in the bad word department.

But then it happened.

One day, I removed the gauze for a short while. Wearing tight bandages for months had rubbed raw places on the skin around my ribs and back and under both arms. So sometimes, I removed all the fuss, wiggled into a freshly laundered gown and allowed my skin a rest. I looked down the neckline and stared at the two flat little skin pockets on my chest.

"Those little skin knobs look absolutely nothing like breasts," I muttered. "But what do they look like? If another woman asked me to describe what these things look like, what would I say?"

For some ridiculous reason, the heads of cats that don't grow fur popped into my head. I have no idea where this thought originated. I have only seen those types of cats in pictures. I don't even know the proper name of the species. But that thought tickled what had been dormant for more than a month: my sense of humor (warped as it is). I started to laugh hysterically, right there alone on my couch. In that moment, those two ugly knobs of skin immediately became known as my "kitty heads."

It was goofy, of course. But friends on Facebook immediately rallied. People left phone messages: "Hi Sherri, I'm just calling to check on you and your kitty heads." They wrote Facebook messages. They posted photos of those ugly cats, naked of fur. And every time a person made reference to my kitty heads, I found it funny all over again.

That's when I started to laugh a lot more and cry a lot less. I had finally discovered a way to laugh at my very unfunny situation. And the best part about it? Other people helped to lighten my heart. They helped me find and hold onto humor again. I am very sure that jokes and silly comments about my kitty heads carried me the rest of the way. I learned that even when I felt absolutely awful, I never felt so bad that I couldn't laugh. What a gift that was!

January 2014

I made little boob cupcakes. Chocolate with pink icing and half of a maraschino cherry in the middle as a nipple. Then I surprised everyone at the comedy writer's group.

I dearly love the people there. We always laugh. We always encourage each other. I never have to be anyone except me.

Walking in unannounced was hard for me. Their eyes filled with tears and so did mine.

I am so blessed to know the people in this group. They sent me one of my favorite cards, ever. Every time I opened it, I felt cared about.

They seemed to like the cupcakes, too!

January 2014

This morning, I saw the breast surgeon. Her first comment was, "Don't you look better, Miss Sherri!"

She said I have more color in my face. I'm not as pasty.

She said my eyes look better. Not as tired.

While the sweet surgeon tossed compliments in my direction, I hoped she would finish off the awesome visit by announcing that I can now step into the shower.

I have not had a shower since Dec. 2, 2013, the morning of the mastectomy. During that shower, I bawled my face off and watched water drip off the breasts that would be cut off my chest.

Because it puts too much pressure on the incisions, I cannot lean forward and wash my hair in the sink. When I couldn't drive and felt too weak to walk there, I took a taxi to the hair salon.

I can lean back to get my hair washed, as long as the stylist hurries so I don't have to be in that position too long. At least I can feel good about having clean hair. And I leave the salon with wet hair, partly because I am too cheap to pay $25 for a blow dry and partly because I want to dry my own hair. It is just another baby step toward normal.

But these little "spit baths" as my grandma would have called them got old a long time ago.

Sometimes I wonder about how it will feel to get in the shower the first time with no breasts.

The new incisions are healing well, but they are not yet closed. So there's no shower in my future until that happens. The risk of infection is too high.

I still have to change the dressing three times daily and keep damp gauze on the unhealed areas.

Today, the surgeon snipped away at some areas around the unhealed incisions. Since I have no sensation in most areas of my chest, I couldn't feel the snips. And that was a good thing.

105

But then she snipped at a different stitch and that one I definitely felt. In fact, I felt it so much that I almost peed my pants.

January 2014

All the way to the doctor's office, I told myself, "If she says you can't take a shower, don't cry."

She was so happy with how well my last incision healed that my awesome doctor smiled at me and said, "Well, it looks like you can get in the shower now!"

And guess what? I cried.

I still have to wear all the bandages. But I don't have to come back here for two weeks!

That is amazing news since I feel like I have been driving to the doctor's office every Monday for at least 11 years!

From the good doctor's office, I went to see my sweet friend Ronnie. She is an artist and such a funny humor writer. Within just a few minutes we were all caught up in this shrieking, hysterical laughter ... the kind that coats your bruised-up soul with all kinds of sweet stuff.

We laughed our way through a nice lunch. Then we stopped by a mastectomy boutique.

To tell you the truth, I was apprehensive about going inside. I didn't want the happy to drip out of my day by being around a bunch of paraphernalia for boobless women.

I didn't try anything on. I wasn't in the mood to lift my arms and worry about bandages, especially since I only had one extra bandage in my purse.

After spending time with Ronnie, I drove out to Pine Island for the writers meeting. But I got there early and promptly stretched out on Gail's couch. I was so tired that I felt like crying.

This was the first day that I crammed in lots of sitting and driving and getting in and out of the car ... which pulls on the muscles on my left side.

Seeing everyone at the meeting was nice, too. It feels like I am "back" from a long, long journey.

Chapter Nineteen

Standing under hot water that first time made my entire body sigh. I stayed in there until the water ran cold. Unfortunately, the forest growing on my legs remained untouched. Leaning forward to shave my legs put too much pressure on my little kitty heads.

I didn't mind if the hair on my legs got long enough to braid. I just wanted to feel clean. For several days in a row, I took at least two showers every day, sometimes three.

As the weeks went by, the swelling around my chest subsided. Soon, the incisions would be healed enough that I wouldn't have to wear bandages anymore. So I looked through my closet, which was filled with V-neck tops. By watching "What Not to Wear," I learned that V-neck everything would best camouflage my former chest full of boobs. But now I didn't feel comfortable in most of my clothing. Most of the tops were too big. The V-neck helped magnify the fact that my chest was flat as a flitter.

"You look like the poster child for bilateral mastectomy," I groaned at my reflection.

It took a while to again open the drawer where I kept my bras. I did not want to deal with the big fat Niagara-style sobbing that happened the last time I saw a bra I no longer needed. Even looking at those articles of clothing that were of no use to me anymore, well, it broke my heart. So I decided to leave that part alone. Time would step in between my bras and me. I trusted that I would eventually get to a place where I could deal with my underwear drawer without a freak-out festival.

I decided to stay in the happy of what was going well. And actually, lots of things were going well: I could drive myself to the weekly doctor appointments; I could drive to the grocery store, even though I also had to go every other day since I could not lift very much; I was allowed to shower again. And sometimes, I slept longer.

Jan. 29, 2014

I posted on Facebook that I was giving away my bras. And then I decided to be a big girl, stuff the bras in manila envelopes to send to other women who could use them and stop being a baby.

Then I drove to the post office, wearing the T-shirt that my friend Gail bought me. It says, "Heck yes they are fake. The real ones tried to kill me."

I was feeling very proud of the fact that I had jumped another hurdle until the lady behind the counter asked if there was anything perishable or hazardous in the packages. When my eyes filled up with fat monster tears, I was horrified. As she stared at me, I felt the need to explain why I was apparently on my way to a meltdown in the middle of the post office.

"I am sending my bras to my friends," I barely said it.

I thought about adding, "And to answer your question, no, none of the items are infected with breast cancer."

The woman reached across the counter and took my hands in hers. "Bless you, Sweetie."

Well I barely made it back to my car. I laid my head on the steering wheel and cried.

The pain of this experience is always just below the surface of my breath.

Just when I think to myself, "Okay, I'm good now. I'm past all the bad stuff," I crack up again.

I went home and got back in my pajamas.

I only wanted to deal with myself for the rest of the day. Just avoid any moment that would conjure up a big batch of unexpected tears.

But I will get through this. I will make it to the other side.

February 2014

This morning, I took an unintentional stroll through anatomy class.

When I decided to venture past my driveway, it was already hot and humid. But I made my way toward the beach since there's almost always a breeze off the water.

First, I envied the self-esteem of a woman with an enormous set of knockers. She had some serious self-confidence, to jog past me with those monster mammary glands bouncing all over the place.

Those nipples were the size of 10p nails. And I'm not joking!

My mind shouted, "May day! May day! That giant boob will put your eye out!"

All I wanted was for that woman and the boobs with their own address to get past me without injury.

A few steps up the beach, another female jogger appeared. As she passed me, it was impossible not to notice that six yards of Spandex had taken up residence in the crack of her hind end.

Now don't tell me she couldn't feel that! Somewhere along the way, she had to notice some discomfort.

"Oh my gosh," she might have thought to herself. "My ass is

111

apparently trying to eat my shorts! I should tend to this problem, if not for myself then for the innocent beach walkers behind me!"

Well, I naively decided that once she was out of my line of vision, I could forget the experience, much like flipping the TV channel.

But oh I was wrong. So, so wrong.

The woman jogged a bit farther, turned around and headed back in my direction.

And that's when I saw, shining in the sun like a beacon ... the perfect outline of her abnormally large and loose labia.

That thing worked like a fan for her sweaty legs ... a personal genital fan.

I fought the urge to snap, "No one wants to see your enormous cooch! Now cover that freak of nature!"

I promise that lady's you-know-what looked like an extra forehead!

When I turned to head home, I was again visually assaulted.

"Well I'll be damned," I whispered under my breath.

He was wearing a Speedo, of course. And I could not stop my eyes from staring at the older man's big, long testicles. How in the world did that happen? Do all aging men deal with those long banana balls? Yuck.

For just a moment or two, my inner freak began to nag at me. I considered ripping off my shirt and all the bandages to show off my kitty heads.

Nah ... maybe tomorrow.

February 2014

Last night, Elaine and I talked for a long time on the phone. I told her that I can feel a few ways that breast cancer has changed me.

Now that doesn't mean that I'll be wearing Peter Pan collars with plaid and pearls.

I don't intend to remove my nose piercing and start dating Republicans, either.

The changes I see in myself are nothing like that stuff. These changes are deeper.

Even though I still wrestle with sudden sobbing, I absolutely know that breast cancer brought me more confidence.

Now I often say to myself, "If I can live through this, then of course I can do that." And whatever "that" turns out to be, I'm very sure I will be strong enough to face it.

I feel a new lightness in my chest. It is an odd, centered feeling I have not experienced for at least 30 years ... or maybe ever.

It is a soft feeling, and it is guiding me and whispering to me, from one day to the next.

I am beginning to forgive myself for all the bad marriages. Those were bricks on my back that I no longer want to carry.

February 2014

Every single time I go in the office, there's a knot in my stomach. But today's appointment with the surgeon went really well!!

Incisions on the left side are completely healed!

On the right side, a scab the size of my thumb nail is still not healed. So I have to wear the bandages another week.

If everything looks okay at the next appointment, then reconstruction begins. I am afraid of that step. But excited, too. It is a new move toward normal.

I wanted to make a plan for spring, to see my son and daughter-in-law and so many other people I love so much. But unfortunately, I can't make a plan for anything.

I am still restricted from lifting anything over five pounds. I have to see the doctor every Monday. And when the saline injections start, the doctor says the process will be slow.

My gynecologist spoke with me about removing my last ovary. But not until my body has had a chance to regain some strength from these other surgeries. Some parts of this process have tried me on every level.

Losing breasts is awful. Growing pretend ones isn't any fun, either! Ha!

But I am on the home stretch now.

February 2014

Once again, medically created nipples were discussed with me. The material for creating the nipple would likely be taken from my vagina.

Just the thought of it makes me cringe.

How much hell would that be? Kitty heads screaming on my chest while my poor old hoo-ha stung like crazy.

Oh hell no.

My lady parts are the only areas that don't hurt, thank you very much. No spelunking will be allowed in my private stuff.

114

Today when I examined my chest, I saw the slightest little jiggle of the kitty heads. And I started to cry and laugh at the same time. The new skin is wrinkly and pliable. I am growing enough elastic to cover those implants one of these days.

February 2014

Hmm. I was just thinking about the fact that fat guys have more boobs than I do. AND they have nipples!

Even when I had boobs, I didn't understand why females are required to wear tops at the beach.

Now that I don't have breasts and I don't have nipples, either, shouldn't I go topless?

I wonder how much trouble I would get in if I tested my theory.

February 2014

I saw the oncologist today. And he saw the kitty heads. Thank goodness he said I am healing well.

"You made a brave decision, a difficult decision," he said of the mastectomy. "You obviously made the right decision, too."

I smiled even though I was temporarily blinded by tears. "So that's it?"

"No, I will see you again in six months," he said.

Damn it.

I wanted to stop spending most of my life hanging around with everything related to breast cancer.

When I got to my car, I opened the lab report from the

mastectomy. Right there in black and write, the pathology reports noted lobular cancer in my other breast.

All over again, I am so thankful that I listened to my intuition.

February 2014

For a few weeks now, I've left a card with a letter inside of it on top of a stack of other cards and letters.

I've left it easily accessible to read again, to think about.

In the letter, that person expressed that she was upset with me for not answering her calls.

She said that until I got breast cancer, she thought we were better friends than that. She thought I would at least pick up the phone and call her back later.

But I didn't.

When I review the letter, I think again about apologizing to her. I think about reminding her that I could not talk to anyone, not just her. For weeks, I could not talk.

I think about reminding her that I do not hurt other people on purpose. Ever.

I think about reminding her of the obvious ... that I have never had breast cancer before. I don't know how to do this.

In fact, I am still stumbling around, trying to find my way.

Then I think about saying to her, "This is not about you. This time, it is about me. This time, I am not strong enough to listen to all of your problems."

I decide, for one of the few times in my life, that my needs are also valid.

I decide that I don't have to explain or defend how I feel. I don't need to explain what I do or don't do and why.

The people who really love me and know me and trust me ... well, those people know I will be back in their lives -- when I can be.

They know I love them so much and miss them, too. But I need a minute to get myself back together.

In that moment, I decide that I will never answer that letter. I will let go of that friendship.

I don't want lopsided friendships anymore, with me being the one to hurry up and breastfeed whoever happens to be in crisis.

I don't have nipples anymore. That's my hint, I think, to make some changes in my life and start weaning some people who take, take and take.

With peace in my heart, I let go of that letter. And don't look back.

I am retired now from breastfeeding other people.

Chapter Twenty

September of 2013 was the last time I was in Indiana. I flew up there for the annual party at the farm. That big party is something my dad and uncles look forward to hosting every year. They love to mow the fields and hitch wagons to a couple of the tractors. They take a lot of pride in providing hay rides for family members, neighbors and friends.

It meant a lot to me that my dad wanted me to be there each year. And I was very happy that I went. There was no way to know it at the time, of course. But two months later, breast cancer showed up. And so, that party at the farm was the last time I saw my son and daughter-in-law and lots of friends I love so dearly.

In January and February, a couple of aunts and uncles from Indiana visited Florida and invited me out for dinner. When they commented that I looked great, I was thrilled. I still wasn't sleeping well and still struggled to get back my energy, still struggled with pain. But as long as other people couldn't see those issues by simply looking at me, I was happy with that.

I tried to look like I was doing a lot better than I was. I didn't want anyone to worry. I didn't want my parents to think they needed to give up their lives again and come back to Florida. But when Elaine came to visit for a week, I didn't need to pretend that I was training for a triathlon. A lot of times, it's true that you can be who you really are with friends much easier than you can with family. We spent a lot of time just quietly catching up on the back porch. She also rearranged a lot of things for me, so I could get to them easier.

In February, I decided I was strong enough to support my

friend Kat during her first art show in Naples. To be honest, I was nervous about driving that far. But I also told myself to stop being such a pansy. However, I failed to remember that while I was at home or at the doctor's office every week, completely submerged in all things breast cancer, snow birds were flocking to both Lee County and Collier County. I was shocked to find myself in the middle of bumper-to-bumper traffic. To make matters worse, quite a few drivers did not seem to have a clue about where they were headed. At one point, the person in front of me just suddenly stopped moving in the middle of a green light. To avoid crashing into the back of her car, I stomped on my brakes. The road was a little bit slick from rain and my car slid sideways, missing her bumper by inches.

The experience felt like it happened in slow motion. The only thought in my head was, "Please God, don't let the air bags go off at impact."

The vision of the air bag exploding on my tender chest made me feel sick. And the near miss upset me so much that I had to pull off the road. For a few minutes, I rested my head on the steering wheel, trying to slow my heartbeat. I reminded myself that everything was okay, that the experience was only close to being a collision. I should get my act together and keep moving. But it was very difficult to continue the drive to Naples. My confidence was shot.

Apparently, I also pulled a muscle on my right side from tensing up. It started to throb. What I wanted more than anything was to turn my car around and go home. But I forced myself to go. As I was leaving the event, I pressed my right hand across my chest and tried to back out of the very tight parking space since maneuvering the wheel caused my chest to feel pressured and painful. Someone behind my car suddenly honked continuously, impatiently waiting for me to give them my space. First, I thought about just spending the night right there in the parking lot so they couldn't get their way. Then my eyes filled with tears. An anxiety attack began to bubble in my throat. I wasn't sure I could back out of the parking space without losing my damn mind. Then my head filled up with red-hot anger.

"Shut up, you rat bastard," I yelled in my car. "I'm doing the best I can."

But the honking continued. And before I knew it, I angrily threw my car into park and slid out of the seat, ready to beat the dog shit out of whoever was blasting their horn at me.

Wow. It was a fancy car filled with four obviously wealthy, snotty women.

"You need to back up so I can back out," I said stiffly.

All of them glared at me. So I used the moment, hoping to do a little bit of breast cancer education right there in the parking lot.

"I've had a mastectomy," I explained nicely since I wasn't really in the mood to go to jail for assaulting four girly girls with designer everything on their starving, bony bodies. "My chest is still sore."

"Well then you shouldn't be driving," one of them snapped.

"I almost feel bad for all the names we've been calling you," the driver said with a satanic smile.

I thought, but didn't say, "If my chest wasn't screaming, this would be a great night for me to mop the asphalt with your expensive highlights."

"Back up," I said through clenched teeth. And then I added a "please" at the end, since I was trying to restrain myself from reaching inside that car to blindly slap at the Botox.

A few days later, I realized that sliding on the wet pavement fed that anxiety that already brewed in other areas of my life. All of a sudden, I could not drive in the rain. I absolutely could not do it. That phobia stayed with me until early July. I was absolutely terrified of being involved in a car accident. If rain was in the forecast, I missed writers meetings. I cancelled plans at the last minute with friends. It was embarrassing and debilitating, too.

My ability to work through challenges was no longer what it was before breast cancer. Every time a minor something occurred, I went to pieces. I started to worry about whether I could ever find a way to navigate the rest of the way through all things pink. I was turning into a frazzled ball of nerve endings. But I didn't know how to fix any of it. I was too humiliated to talk about it. My mind was beginning to imprison the rest of me. And that thought scared me to death. When it rained, I started forcing myself to drive down the street. But I couldn't drive any farther. I couldn't get my breath. My whole body was trembling.

Along with the driving phobia, I still couldn't sleep in my bed. When I got on the bed, I felt like I was smothering. Daily, I reminded myself that I wasn't a total nut cake. In other ways, I could now do lots of things I couldn't do two weeks ago or a month ago. I reminded myself that losing my mind just because I lost my breasts did not make a damn bit of sense.

February 2014

Several friends of mine don't really attach themselves to a culture. Many of them grew up in cookie-cutter houses in the suburbs of large cities. Some have a few faint memories of visiting grandparents or aunts and uncles who farmed or at least lived life on a narrow country road.

My family background is filled with the simplistic beauty of country-loving people.

I grew up hearing my dad say, "They don't make more land, you know," in reference to so many examples of big-city types who have no respect for fields of soybeans or corn.

I know the scent of fresh-cut hay. I love the sound of an old tractor being fired up.

I love my Southern roots as much as I love words.

Strong blood pumps through my veins. Why in the world would I ever doubt that I can't get through the rest of this chapter with breast cancer? Of course I can somehow overcome this anxiety problem. Of course I can do this.

Chapter Twenty-One

In the last week of February, I was introduced to the next phase of recovery. Breast reconstruction officially began. This process included weekly injections of saline, which I referred to as build-a-boob sessions. During those visits, small doses of saline were injected through a monster needle into the port on each side of my rib cage. From the port, the saline traveled through a tube inside my body to miraculously settle inside the funny-looking little kitty heads.

But during the first procedure, the doctor discovered that both ports had flipped upside down under my skin.

Because of the second and very unplanned surgery in mid-December, all other procedures had been delayed. So the ports had been left inside my body for a lot longer than originally planned, from Dec. 2, 2013, to late February 2014. That meant the ports had to be manually flipped.

As my doctor pressed on my ribcage, moving the ports under my skin with her hands, it hurt so much that it literally took my breath. I broke out in a sweat, feeling like I might vomit all over the place. Anxiety rippled up the back of my neck, and I didn't know whether I felt more like sobbing or screaming. Thankfully, she got the ports flipped back to where they were supposed to be. Even with numbing solution, the needle stung like crazy when it punctured my skin. As the saline was slowly injected into the tube, it felt like a week went by.

For several days afterward, the injection of saline stretched the skin, making it difficult to walk and move. The slightest jarring of my chest put me in tears. Opening and closing the car door was unpleasant, to say the least. Sleeping was out of the question. I ached all over. I could not lie flat on my back since it brought on the sensation that someone had placed a boat on my kitty heads.

By the time I finally felt better, it was Monday again. Time to drive back to the surgeon's office, clench my teeth and go through the procedure all over again.

It was very wearing. And I was reminded once again how tired I was. In fact, by that time, I was traveling on empty. Many days, I just barely got one foot in front of the other, trying to get through these next weeks of breast reconstruction.

Before the mastectomy, the plastic surgeon said I was an excellent candidate for implants. Then we discussed what breast size I would like to be when I could finally get the implants. At that time, I told her that I would like to get to a size C. It was perfectly okay with me that I would never again be a double D. Those pups were difficult to clothe, always gapping buttons on blouses. They were difficult to carry around, too. And the perk of losing my breasts was that my neck and back troubles decreased a little bit by lightening my load. The other perk was that I would never again have to live my life in underwire bras.

At the time that I said I wanted to be a C cup, I was only thinking about the shock I still felt when I looked in the mirror at a flat chest. I reasoned that getting a C cup would ease that feeling. But of course, that was long before I found out what was involved with the weekly build-a-boob sessions.

When I was introduced to reconstruction, I decided that a little bitty B cup would make me just as happy. I would go with a B cup, so I had a little something under clothes. I would go with a B cup because I realized that boobs were not nearly as important to me as I thought. I wanted to take the fast track through breast reconstruction. It was too painful and trying.

Most of all, breast cancer still had my life in a holding

pattern. And I didn't like that. Not one bit.

March 3, 2014

I got in the car this morning to drive to the build-a-boob session and immediately realized some problems. The CD would not eject or stop playing. The seat warmer wouldn't work, either.

I was already scared to death of the doctor visit. So car trouble caused me some hysteria.

I called my friend Tammy, who offered to meet me at the doctor's office. But I didn't want her to drive that distance unless the car battery was dead after my appointment.

Then I cried because she offered to drop everything and be there for me. I am so thankful to have such loving people in my life.

I called Elaine, whose husband Rick is an amazing mechanic. We made a plan that Rick would try to talk me through some ways to fix the problem. But first, I had to get through the doctor appointment.

I finished the long drive from the beach to Cape Coral, bawling my head off and deciding that I was getting too old to go through these moments alone.

Thankfully, things went so much better this time! The ports had not flipped over again between last week and this week.

With new strength, I walked back out to the car with the never-ending CD still playing and it started right up, thank God. Then I turned it off and on again two more times. Who knows how it happened. The only part that matters is that I somehow got the CD to shut off.

Crisis averted.

At home, I lifted my blouse, removed the bandages and happily inspected my chest. With this new saline injection, my kitty heads look a little more fluffed and puffy. They are actually kind of cute.

Chapter Twenty-Two

I am still thinking about a late-night conversation with my aunt, the one who was the first in our family to have breast cancer. She has insomnia like me. So it isn't strange at all for one of us to call the other sometime after midnight. Those are the hours when I like to work. That's when my aunt likes to watch TV and look through old pictures of her life.

On that particular night, she shared with me how deeply hurt she was all those years ago to face breast cancer without a husband. She truly understood how hard this entire experience has been for me. A few months before her diagnosis, my aunt's marriage of more than twenty years abruptly ended. Like so many women in her age group, she had left her parents' home and moved directly into a marriage. She had never lived alone or worked outside the family business. Just when her future was turned upside down, breast cancer struck.

Since the mastectomy, she never even entertained the possibility of remarrying. But that night on the phone, she encouraged me not to follow in her footsteps. She reminded me that somehow, I had to make peace with how my chest looks now. She assured me that someday a good man would cross my path and never care one bit about the fact that I no longer have breasts.

"Don't be like me, Sherri Lynn," my aunt said. "I'm in my seventies and the grandchildren are all grown up now. It's really lonely. You can't imagine how lonely it is. Don't be like me."

As she sobbed on the other end of the phone that night, I wondered if this was maybe one of the few times, if any, when my aunt felt safe enough to truly let her guard down. All of her feelings were still so vivid, even after all these years. Her pain rushed out, like slivers of glass across her heart. We both cried a lot during that phone call. I didn't tell her that I am already exactly like her. I didn't tell her that long before the breast cancer, I was already terrified of ever trying again to love a man. I left out that part, along with the fact that I would likely use a mastectomy as the perfect excuse for why I wanted to just be left the hell alone.

With other family members, I keep my guard so high they can't even see my eyes. But it was not embarrassing to talk about the unbelievable ache in my heart, for how my body is forever scarred. I didn't need to reel my heart in for the sake of another person. My aunt was not surprised by any of the thoughts and feelings I shared with her. She had experienced all of them herself. Even though she was in Kentucky and I was in Florida, we talked as if we were sitting across from each other in the same room.

After we said goodbye, I sat on the porch until the sun came up, thinking about how breast cancer stole so much more from my aunt than her breasts. I thought about how much better my scars look than hers. With thirty years of research and experience, surgeons have developed more skill in the removal of breasts. But it's still not enough to keep me from swallowing hard and blinking a million times when I see my chest in the mirror. So I could never know how my aunt has felt for all of these years, never wanting a man to see her chest. I wished for both of us that we could get to a place where unbuttoning a blouse in front of a man led to strong, brave words like, "This is what my courage looks like. Right here. Where my breasts used to be. This is my fight. And it is sometimes difficult to look at. Yet on other days, these scars are beautiful. They remind me of what I am willing to go through, just to stay in the world."

With big hot tears dripping off my chin, I closed my eyes and prayed, "God, please don't let me feel shame about this. Don't let me get to that place, where I feel like I am less of a woman. I have nothing to be humiliated about. I know that. So please don't let me ever question who I am as a woman just because I have no breasts."

Chapter Twenty-Three

Four days after the second injection of saline, I decided to participate in a book fair in downtown Fort Myers. I would share a table with my friends from Pine Island Writers. But I knew it would be a big test. I had to be in Fort Myers by 7:30 in the morning, which meant that I had to make a few hundred trips to the car with books since I wasn't allowed to lift more than five pounds. I also had to leave home around 6:30 that morning, knowing that I had to sit up all day.

I had no sleep the night before the book fair. As usual, the skin expanders hurt all damn night. Sometimes (okay, most of the time), I can be way too stubborn. This was one of those times. I forced myself to go to the book fair even though I already felt like hell. I could not stand the thought of missing an opportunity to connect with women and talk about my mission with my books.

Long before noon, I knew I had made a bad decision. My back was absolutely screaming from sitting in the chair for so long. The incisions on my chest throbbed. But because I will also never win awards for common sense, I was too proud to throw in the towel and go home early. A few women who bought books from me last year showed up again, which thrilled me! They were so excited that this year, I had a new book for them, *Hissy Fits Set you Free*. For a few hours, that excitement convinced me that I could make it until it was time to shut everything down. By the way, shutting everything down included carrying all the boxes out of the building, across the street and up the parking garage elevator.

I still don't know why it was so damn important to me to pretend I was fine when I obviously was not. But as I said, pride gets in my way as often as stubborn moments do. It always has, actually. And on that day, I gave an award-winning performance for everyone around me. I knew that every single one of the people at our table would understand if I said I had to go home. But I didn't want to lose the chance to sell my books. And I didn't want to admit that breast cancer was kicking my ass once again, either.

Since my parents were in Florida that week but planned to leave the next morning for Indiana, I put myself through even more hell by agreeing to meet them for dinner after the book festival. I didn't want to hurt their feelings by not going. I also didn't want them to know that I felt so horrible. I didn't want them to worry. I was in so much pain that my stomach was upset. But I do not take pain pills when I drive. And so, by the time I got home that evening, my only goal in life was to swallow the pain meds and recover from my long day. I didn't plan on bawling my head off about it, but the frustrated tears came anyway. So my head got to hurt as much as my incisions and my back. That was on a Saturday. I would have to muster every single ounce of energy to get through Monday's reconstruction visit.

A few Monday mornings later, back on the Cape as usual for yet another build-a-boob session, my doctor studied me for a long moment. I knew that I looked and felt like a worn-out mop. But when a nurse took my blood pressure, my world got even more difficult. The doctor described my blood pressure reading as "stroke level."

Great.

I had a flat chest and felt awful, too. Now I had to also worry about having a stroke?

I started to cry. It was certainly not a moment that I'm proud of but big, snotty sobs that come from absolutely feeling beat down and exhausted and hurt and scared took over. My doctor sat down with me while I bent all the way over, with my hands over my face, completely losing my damn mind. She explained that stress and continuous pain could be the culprit for the blood pressure issue. And it could kill me if I didn't get a handle on things.

I got myself together enough to make one of my smart-ass cracks, that maybe I should take up drinking. But the doctor wasn't amused. I left her office with a prescription for blood pressure medicine. The counter in my kitchen already looked like a pharmacy, so I suppose one more pill bottle wouldn't be a big deal. I was starting to realize though that I had to find a way to shut my mind down. I constantly felt guilty about my family helping me financially. I felt like a loser. I wanted so badly to get back on my feet. I wanted to be independent. I wanted to feel like my life was coming back to me. But now another, equally serious health issue had arrived and unpacked, right on top of my very fragile psyche.

Once I got home, I sat down to regroup. Less than three months had gone by since the second surgery. I had only begun the reconstruction process. I was still weak. Still foggy from anesthetic. Still overwhelmed by sudden crying spells and lack of sleep. Still dealing with skin expanders and ports and pain.

"Okay, God," I said, more than once during those days and weeks of trying to get the blood pressure down. "Okay, I get it. I will do my best to stay away from stress. I will do my best to recognize all that I can't change about so many things in my life."

I did what the doctor asked me to do. I rested and napped. I stopped trying to push myself so much. Very quietly, I faced the fact that I was not physically ready to do anything more. I was mad about it, but I tried my best to accept exactly where I was and what I had to do now, to feel better. It was difficult, though. It scared me, to feel like I was giving in. But it was time to stop pretending that I was in control.

March 2014

My stomach has been jittery since yesterday, dreading today's appointment with the breast surgeon.

If the port has somehow flipped over again this week, I will jump off that exam table and slam the door on my head a few times until I knock myself out.

And THEN, she can get busy breaking my ribs again to flip the ports back into place.

I've had it now with a thousand doctor appointments and long nights and pain pills.

I might come unglued and be a big baby for a while, but I always manage to get myself back together.

I walk into her office, thinking, "I can do this another time."

All bets are off, though, when I get safely out the door.

Last week, for example, I couldn't even hold it together until I got to my car. I lost my mind in the bathroom.

My nerves ... Oh God, my nerves are shot.

March 2014

To get through the very uncomfortable doctor visits, I'm trying to perfect this weird little self-hypnosis approach. So this morning, I got up extra early, sat in the dark on the porch and practiced deep breathing.

As I drove across the Cape Coral bridge, I tried to get into that calm zone. It's an extension of the way I try to get myself ready in the waiting room before my name is called.

I dreaded another reconstruction appointment. Both ports are so sore and sensitive from being jabbed with that monster needle.

But I managed to concentrate on staying calm. I didn't cry! Not during the procedure and not in the car on the way home. No snotty moments.

I am definitely on to something. And so, if I can perfect this, maybe I can one day master meditation.

Meditation, by the way, scares me to death. Sometimes I worry that my mind would drift too far out of my head and forget to come back.

Got stuck in snowbird traffic on the bridge, which meant my pain meds were more than an hour overdue.

By the time I made it home, I felt like someone parked their car on my chest.

But I still went straight to the bathroom mirror, raised up my shirt and smiled at those itty bitty kitty heads. They are definitely beginning to bloom. They are round and compact. But I wouldn't care if they looked like bananas.

Just stay healthy. That's the goal.

I now have a total of 275 cc of saline, which means I am halfway to the finish line -- at least with the build-a-boob steps.

Using two models, the nurse showed me today the differences between saline implants and silicone implants.

Because I have no breast tissue and an issue with healing, the doctor suggests silicone.

I trust her judgment. And so, when I go back to surgery to remove the expanders and ports, two saline implants will be placed in the sockets where my breasts were.

Every two years, I will need to undergo an MRI to make sure the silicone is not leaking.

I wanted to go to the writer's group tonight on Pine Island. But unfortunately, the group meets every Monday. And every Monday morning, I have reconstruction, which means that I feel awful until Saturday afternoon.

On Sunday, I try to get laundry done and groceries in the house before Monday comes around again.

Right now, the kitty heads feel like they swallowed a couple of dump trucks filled with sand.

March 2014

Whoa, what a long night with my chest.

These little kitty heads apparently didn't like yesterday's extra bit of saline injection.

Off and on all night, the ports woke me up with that very familiar stinging, like someone caught my very unsexy nightshirt on fire.

My chest ached all night, too. Felt like it was being squeezed by a trash compactor.

At one point in the night, I actually slept long enough to dream that I was lost on a narrow, curvy road.

I backed into a clearing to turn my car around, but it wouldn't budge. Then I discovered that my car was teetering on the edge of a cliff.

In the dream, it was getting dark. My cell phone wouldn't work. I was afraid to start walking, in the middle of nowhere. I was afraid to get back inside my car since it might fall over the side of the cliff.

I woke up with my heart beating out of my damn chest.

I watched some reruns of Ru Paul's Drag Race. I happen to love drag queens. Such fun guys with the sweetest hearts.

On these nights, I try so hard to avoid it. But sometimes I start to unravel. It is eating me up that my parents are still helping with my bills. This hole I am in just seems to get deeper.

I pour my heart out to God. Thank goodness He is willing to listen to me at 3 a.m.

Today, I will try not to use my peripheral vision. If I look on either side of my life, all I see are these huge mountains of problems that I can't seem to fix.

Today, I will focus on the good. And there IS a lot of good.

March 2014

Well the blood pressure problem still isn't under control. So now I have added a blood pressure cuff to the kitchen counter, which already looks like a pharmacy shelf.

Three times every day, I have to record my blood pressure.

Sometimes I forget that I am 54 years old.

Occasionally I even forget that I have been to hell and back more than a few times in my life.

March 2014

Of course I set myself up for it by making bad jokes about my marital drama. But the truth is that for right now anyway, I don't want to be teased anymore.

It isn't cute to hear, "Sherri, are you working on husband number four?" "Sherri, have you picked out a new victim?"

I also don't want unsolicited advice from females who have absolutely no clue what it is like to live solo. Their advice -- such as, "Your best bet is to just live alone. Haven't you already proven to yourself that you can't be successful in relationships?" -- makes me want to apply duct tape to their lips.

And here's another great one, always from a woman who has been married forever: "If something ever happens with my husband, I will never get married again."

Funny how that advice rolls off the tongues of women who know nothing about living alone.

Sometimes I want to point that out to them.

I want to say that I know they are not strong enough to live like I do.

I know that 20 minutes after they were divorced or widowed, they would be in a panic to find another man. They don't have the skills to keep everything in life rolling along with only one pair of hands.

But instead, I just smile. Who am I to blast their fantasy? They think they know so much.

But I know differently.

Only strong women survive out here in the world alone.

If you manage to make ends meet, that's usually all you've got. I have been blessed to live rent-free in my parents' properties, but even with that very appreciated gift, I have always been broke. You just can't make it alone on one income and expect to get ahead if you don't have a very lucrative career.

Vacations or new clothes are not a common part of life alone.

There's just no money for those extras because you have to save to pay car insurance and doctor bills, etc.

To be alone, you've got to meet your own needs, financially, emotionally and spiritually.

It hurts not to have anyone to share a laugh with.

It's lonely, night after night, to sit alone to watch TV and then sleep alone, too.

Not having anyone to bring you some Sprite or soup when you are sick as a dog doesn't feel very good, either.

When you are single, you've got to know when to turn off the daydreams. For example, on bad days, when I can hardly get my breath, I stop myself from dreaming about traveling or buying my own home or experiencing things I have always wanted to see, such as the Northern Lights and Niagara Falls.

When my heart feels extra heavy, lonely and unloved, I know that I can't dream.

It will just hurt too much.

Being alone also has gifts, though.

Doing exactly as you please all the time is nice.

Not being responsible for someone else's feelings is also a positive.

Also, I think I can hear God much more clearly when my world is silent.

Except for my own voice and God's whisper, that's all I hear, for days and days in a row. Sometimes that truth brings me comfort. Other times, it breaks my heart.

141

March 2014

Most of the time, I love to be in the company of outspoken women.

But lately, I find myself feeling more than a little bit irritated by a few know-it-all remarks.

Like the married women who are so quick to tell me how to live single, a few women who still have breasts on their chests suddenly become experts about how to deal with mastectomy.

"Well they were just breasts. Who needs them? They just got in the way," and "You'll have new little boobs. And the most important part is that you're cancer-free!"

I understand that the majority of those comments are meant to be kind. To be light and encouraging.

Sometimes I can let it go.

But other times, I have to bite my tongue off to keep from saying, "Shut your damn mouth."

I know what I'm talking about. Before Nov. 5, 2013, I was one of those know-it-alls.

I told myself for years that if I ever had to deal with breast cancer, I would do so gracefully .

I'm sure I believed all those thoughts about how strong and brave I would be.

But when the diagnosis was mine, I hit the ground face first.

I don't care who she is, there is not a woman in the world who will honestly say, "Well, they're just breasts," if she knows that hers will soon be whacked off her chest.

This trip through pink is about me.

And so, unless a woman's shoes have been in the same mud as mine, meaning that her chest is just as flat as mine, she knows absolutely nothing about how I should feel or think.

It is an insult to hear, "Well, they were just breasts."

I don't want to hear that sentence unless it's coming from a woman who has no breasts. We are the only ones who get to say, "Well, they were just breasts."

Chances are, we will never say that.

March 2014

I still don't view the kitty heads as breasts.

Wrinkles, gray hair or moles, well, those occurrences feel like they belong with me. They might be new in town, but I know I share their address.

I don't have that feeling about these little skin pockets on my chest. These are foreign objects. I am not emotionally connected to them at all.

And in a way, I am worried about that. I secretly tell myself that I probably should find a way to want these weird little knobs to hang around with me.

For so many years I was painfully self-conscious about my breasts. I would have never yanked up my top to show my big old boobs to anyone.

But these little kitty heads are my traveling show-n-tell for breast cancer.

When women inquire about what my chest looks like, I simply pull up my shirt. And there I am, in the middle of a crash course in bilateral mastectomy.

Like those old public service announcements, "This is your

143

brain on drugs," I am hauling around my own public service message: "This is your chest on breast cancer."

It isn't embarrassing to me, either. Partially because I truly do want to educate women with every opportunity I find.

But also because these little skin nubs are not my breasts.

April 2014

Today I fell in love all over again with that amazing camaraderie of womanhood. With less than an hour to shop before the store closed, I walked into a favorite store in Matlacha with one goal: to find at least one top that I might feel comfortable wearing.

Because a sports bra rides up, rubs on the incisions and will be yanked off and thrown over my shoulder like it's on fire, I don't have many clothing choices at home.

What fits me is too sheer to wear without a sports bra. And nearly everything else is now too big without my double D longs to fill it out.

Finding tops with smaller arm holes has been a task, too ...

Anyway, before I had myself a big, nasty meltdown, I asked the store employee to help me. And wow, she kicked it into high gear.

Just a few minutes later, I was in the dressing room with a small mountain of possibilities.

Then she sent me two doors down and the same thing happened.

I left both stores with new tops.

I also left there with hugs and kisses and tears in my eyes.

I love that my gender shows up.

We do it all the time for each other ... and obviously, women don't find it necessary to even know each other's names. We just dive right into the pain or frustration, and we give it our best shot to bring the other person to a place where they can breathe again.

That is the gift those women gave to me today.

April 2014

Earlier this morning, I accidentally banged my side on the corner of the kitchen counter. That meant that I whacked the port, still floating around on the bottom of my rib cage. It was already very tender to the touch, from being jabbed every Monday with a needle.

So to hit that port ... well, it hurt like hell.

It is still throbbing. Damn it!

At the next surgery, these things will finally be removed. And so, I will definitely show up for that party. Believe me.

The ports still sting like crazy and sometimes get caught between my ribs. The skin expanders continue to beat me to death, too, but the attacks are always by surprise.

A few days ago, I was in the bank, talking to the sweet girls who work in there. And all of a sudden, I felt like someone stuck a knife in my chest.

All of a sudden, I couldn't stand up straight.

I don't have any choice but to breathe through the pain, like a contraction, until it subsides.

Definitely, breast cancer and recovery demand my full

attention at a moment's notice.

Still, I am reminded nearly every day that I am not driving this train. It's about me but then it isn't. Breast cancer shoves my face into the wall of every fear I have ever known and a few I never met.

And then it forces me to slay those bad moments so I can get my damn breath again.

Last night, I was thinking about one of the doctors commenting, "Bilateral mastectomy requires a full year of healing and recovery."

In my head, I had smirked and whispered, "A year? Are you kidding? Breast cancer might steal a year from another woman but not me."

Well, well, well. Guess who is now realizing that I will not be wearing a Super Chick cape any time soon?

Five long-ass months have gone by but still, I can't move around very well at all.

I will undergo a third surgery soon, and if I am not very, very careful, that surgery will only add to my frustration.

Someday when I get to that pink finish line, I intend to dance my ass off.

April 2014

Last night, sweet Michelle, a dear friend and a former co-worker too during my Daily Journal days, called to say she was participating today in the Susan G. Komen breast cancer walk in Indianapolis.

This morning, she sent a text. And there she stood in a pink T-

shirt with "Sherri Strong" printed on the front of it.

I opened Facebook and there she was again, surrounded by a massive sea of pink. Still wearing that T-shirt with my name on it.

I remembered that November day five months ago when I walked into the women's cancer center. It was very difficult to convince myself that I belonged in there.

Everything about anything I ever knew for sure was turned upside down by breast cancer.

This morning, staring at Michelle's picture with my name on her T-shirt, well, that feeling came back to my throat. That feeling of shock and disbelief.

I stared at her smile and like clockwork, I cried and cried.

My hands went to my chest, touched the bandages and fluttered away knowing that yes, I lost my breasts. Yes, I survived this awful disease that kills a woman every 13 minutes of every day.

My friend's participation was such a beautiful, thoughtful gesture. It went straight to my heart. Her life is so busy, filled with so many responsibilities and activities. And yet, Michelle took time to be there, to find a place among thousands of survivors and their loved ones.

I am so blessed to fill my life with such amazing people.

By far, Michelle's presence at the walk is one of the most wonderful gifts anyone has ever given to me.

Thank you, my dear friend, you are walking for so many women. And I dearly love you for that.

Next year, I will be walking, too.

In everything pink.

April 2014

For as long as I can remember, I have always had a weird talent. Like bees to honey, I draw unusual, quirky people.

And people always want to tell me things. Very private and personal things. Most of the time, they don't even know my name. Yet they spill their guts.

So I guess I shouldn't have been the least bit shocked when I walked into a gas station today to pay for gasoline ... and the male attendant shared with me that he will soon undergo a penile implant.

I'm standing there thinking, "Please don't do it. Don't tell me your penis problems."

But he does it anyway. "My doctor said I will be in quite a bit of pain for about a week."

For heaven's sake. It's not even noon. I don't want to envision this guy's dead genitalia.

But then I see agony in his eyes and my heart drops.

He tells me that he has exhausted all efforts with drugs. Nothing has worked. He cannot achieve an erection.

I am grateful that the guy with the sick little soldier and I are the only two people in the gas station.

I feel sorry for him. I don't know what it's like to be a guy with that kind of problem. But why did he pick me to tell about it?

I am thankful that he is standing behind the counter. At least I don't have to fight with my eyeballs.

If he was standing beside me, I am sure I would sneak a glance at his crotch. I wouldn't want to. But that's just how I am. Too curious for my own damn good.

He asks if I know about penile implants. I only shake my head. But the truth is that I haven't seen a live penis in so long, I probably couldn't identify it if someone hit me in the face with one.

"That pump thing is implanted somewhere around my balls," the man says.

Gag.

I don't want to think about his sixty-something-year-old man berries, all shriveled up like raisins.

I don't want to hear another word about the head fallin' off his old hammer. By this age, shouldn't he be finding other activities to engage in? Shuffleboard, maybe?

I manage to wish him luck as I head toward the exit.

"Come back and see me," the man says.

I don't mention that I will never -- not in a kazillion years -- enter this station again.

April 2014

Today I left the surgeon's office with a weird feeling of dread in my chest. It pushed its way into my chest and made me cry.

For some reason, it was just one of those days.

I started to cry and the avalanche came quickly. I cried because the incisions are still too tender and I can't wear a bathing suit or a sports bra. Who knows why I suddenly found that tear-worthy. But I did.

I cried about how humiliated and guilty I felt, to still be so financially dependent on my dad. I cried for the women in my

149

position who don't have a dad to help them.

I cried because I should have applied for disability, to see if I could get some financial assistance instead of putting my dad in this situation to support me for all these months.

It was a nasty crying session, the kind that forces you to close the car windows so other drivers can't hear the wailing at stop lights.

Then I remembered that I am not supposed to do any of what I was doing. For my blood pressure's sake, I was supposed to be as calm as possible.

I got my act together and went to lunch with my friend Tammy. We sat outside in the beautiful sun. We even saw a guy dressed like a super hero, calmly strolling along the downtown sidewalk.

Later, I joined Tammy and her family for an evening of karaoke.

Years ago, I sang in several bands. And I loved it. I still love music. I still love to sing. Sometimes I miss that part of my life.

Lately, I have thought about so many different things I loved for so long but somehow drifted away from doing. Singing is one of those things.

Also, this sweet lady in her eighties came up to our table during karaoke. She introduced herself and told me how much she loves my books. She hugged and kissed me and thanked me for making her laugh.

When she walked away, I whispered a little, "Thank you, God." I realized in those moments that He was tapping my shoulder, reminding me that what I love is worthy. My love for writing books really is a gift to lots of other women.

I loved my day, even the parts that made me cry.

April 23, 2014

I had plans today to ride to Punta Gorde with friends. Then I planned to go this evening to the Comedy Writers group.

But I woke at 5 a.m. with a big fat anxiety attack. Sweating. Panicky. Heart beating out of my chest.

Still wrapped in my blanket, I stepped out on the back porch and sat in the rocker. I tried to decipher what in the world was wrong with me.

That's when I realized that I had to cancel my plans.

I had to stay at home and work toward getting to a more comfortable place.

On Tuesday, I go back to surgery. On Tuesday, these nasty skin expanders and ports will finally be removed. The implants will be placed in the little kitty heads.

Because I write for a living, it is imperative that I have the ability to focus. But when I get stressed, I can't focus. That means I can't write. And when I can't write, I get even more stressed. And that means that I end up skidding very dangerously into deadlines.

That fear of missing deadlines amps up the stress.

Get the picture?

So yes, I had to cancel the plans. Stay home. Be productive. Tackle the long list of things I needed to get done before next Tuesday's surgery date.

The good part is that I know now what I need, in order to make recovery easier. I know I must place nearly everything I use every day on the kitchen counter and the top shelf in the fridge.

On Tuesday, I will once again leave surgery with new incisions. So I will be bumped back to not bending over and not reaching over my head.

I can get organized. I can focus. I can be ready for surgery.

I am doing a much better job of listening to my body.

I am improving the ability to identify what I need to do for myself, in order to avoid feeling emotionally and physically overwhelmed and paralyzed.

I am learning a lot more about how to truly honor myself and my own needs.

April 2014

After I left the surgeon's office today, I sat in my car with the air conditioner blowing on my face. I was in so much pain that I didn't trust myself to drive until I could calm down.

I never know what I will undergo. I never know how I will feel when I leave there. I never know how that evening and night will go, either.

I know that I am overtired. I keep trying to catch up again with life. I want to feel like I have a good hold on something. But I don't.

After I got my act together, I drove to the bank and went inside. An arrogant ass of a man was in there, griping at his elderly mother for "wasting his time."

"I hate that guy," I said to the teller.

She said, "What?"

And I repeated it. Except more loudly this time.

Then I glared in his direction and offered my best "You're just a piece of shit" look.

His face immediately went bright red. And I was thrilled.

Ass.

Happily, I got back in my car. What do I really need to be afraid of? I've been through three awful marriages. I've started over more than anyone I know. I've lost my breasts.

Bring it.

I am not afraid ... of anything except breast cancer.

Chapter Twenty-Four

On the night before surgery, my sweet friend Gail spent the night. We laughed and talked and I tried my best not to even remember that the next morning, I would again be on a surgery table. Even though I was more than ready to get rid of the evil expanders and ports, I was tired of working so hard to build myself up and then be knocked back 17 steps for another recovery.

During my pre-surgery appointment the week before, I asked my doctor to save the torture devices for me to take home. But she looked at me like I had a couple of extra heads. Maybe no one has ever made that request before? Hmmm. I didn't care how nuts it sounded. I truly did want possession of the ports and expanders. After all, they were inside my body from Dec. 2, 2013, to April 29, 2014. I had a history with them! I wanted to maybe wrap them in pink flannel and keep them in a box. On bad days in the future, I planned to peek at those items and remember that I made it through all of this, so I could survive whatever else was difficult. The skin expanders and ports would have also been great additions to my show-n-tell extravaganza with my breastless chest.

At the hospital, I was happy that Ann was again my nurse. She has such a fun personality that it was almost pleasant to be asked once again to change for the third time into the green paper gown.

Almost.

The other perk was the great music playing in the background. So while the nurses stabbed at both arms and the top of my right hand too, trying to start the I.V., I tried to focus on the Motown music instead of my desire to scream and cry. After that little crisis, my nose piercing became the topic of discussion. I repeated the same little baby fit that I threw before the mastectomy and before the second surgery, too. I just flatly refused to remove the piercing.

"I need this," I said very seriously to the nurses. "I can't remove it. I'm sorry."

They assumed the piercing was physically imbedded. And I did nothing to clear up the confusion. But the truth was that I could have removed the piercing. I just didn't want to. I looked at my silly little nose piercing in the same way Wonder Woman viewed her bracelets. Seven months after my third divorce, my daughter-in-law and I made the trek to one of my friends' tattoo studios. I got the piercing to remind myself of my spirit. By the time the breast cancer challenge came around, I was clinging to that sparkly little piercing. I needed it for emotional strength. And so, I removed all of my earrings (three in one ear and two in the other) but left the nose piercing in place.

After the preparations were complete, my surgery was a bit delayed. So I took photos with my phone — of the I.V. taped to the top of my hand, green booties on my feet that sexy green hat on my head, looking like a mushroom stuffed with hair. I posted them on Facebook. What amazing technology! I was waiting for surgery yet I was entertaining myself and preventing another crack-up session by playing around with silly photos on social media.

Later, I learned that some other friends, Nellie and Tammy, showed up in the waiting room to keep Gail company. My cousin Dayna would have also been there, but I totally forgot to give her the address of the surgery center.

That afternoon, Gail brought me home. The surgery went well. Another friend, Judi, showed up to stay the night with me. But I wasn't much company to her. I felt pretty darn rough, to tell you the truth. Because I hadn't slept at all the night before, I went to bed at 10 p.m. An hour later, I was awake. My chest felt like it was on fire. I was crying and pissed at myself. I should have taken the pain pill as it was scheduled. But I didn't think I needed it. Because I had to take the medication with food, I leaned on the kitchen counter with one hand pressed against my chest while I stuffed a naked piece of bread down my throat with the other hand. Still, I was up and down all night. I just needed to remember that eventually, I would have more normalcy than I could remember in the last five months of my life.

April 2014

I took a nap but woke abruptly with my left side killing me. It hurt so badly that I started to cry, cry and cry.

My sweet friend Judi kicked it into nurse mode. She flew to the kitchen to get the pain pills. She sat on the bed with me and patted my hand until I could get myself calmed down. I just love her kind heart.

Thank you, God, for pain medication. And thank you just as much for girlfriends.

When the medicine kicked in, Judi helped me change the gauze. These compression bandages are so uncomfortable. I just remind myself that it won't be long before I don't have to deal with bandages anymore.

Tomorrow, I will try to handle things better than I did today. I let myself get a little bit too tired. I let myself get a little bit too hopeful that this surgery would not put me flat on my back again.

I will work harder on patience.

April 2014

Early this morning, Judi will drive me to the surgeon's office so the incisions can be checked. Bless her sweet heart.

Like Gail, Judi took time away from work and her other responsibilities to help me. I am so blessed with such good friends.

On the way to the doctor's office, I asked her to stop by Publix. I was in so much pain that I was sick. I wanted some Pepto-Bismol to settle my stomach.

I thought the walk from the car to the store might do me some good, too. So I made quite the fashion statement in the grocery store, wearing a pajama top over my once-again heavily bandaged chest. My look was polished off with a too-big pair of capris, the sexy white surgical hose, house shoes and barely brushed hair.

I can't even say how much this didn't bother me. I felt so damn miserable, I didn't care at all who stared at me.

At the doctor's office, my stomach got even more queasy when she slowly unwrapped all the bandages on my very swollen chest. I felt like I might vomit. I didn't want to experience gauze sticking to new incisions. And I sure didn't want to see the finished artwork on my chest.

Save that for a day when I don't feel like dying.

But she stood back and admired her handiwork. "Look how pretty they are, Miss Sherri."

When she handed me a mirror, I couldn't exactly be a big brat by saying, "I have no interest in your artwork."

So I looked ... because I'm a people pleaser from way back.

And suddenly, I was glad that I looked.

These new pretend boobs are kind of adorable. They might be faceless, in regard to the nippleness of the situation. And they are scarred up, like they've been in a bad wreck.

But all in all, they are kind of sweet.

April 2014

Another doctor visit and another big lecture. For eight weeks, I have to basically be a vegetable. I can't walk around much. I'm not supposed to perspire; it can cause bacteria to move into the fresh incisions.

The good stuff is that, when I run my hand along my side, I don't feel those Dr. Frankenstein knobs on my rib cage!

Even though I am so grateful that I no longer have to deal with the wicked skin expanders and the ports from hell, the fresh incisions sting and ache like crazy. And I feel awful.

My sweet friend Tena and her sister Cheryl came to visit. I did not want to feel like a worn-out old rag. I did manage to sit up for quite a while and talk with them.

But I fell asleep at 8:30 p.m., party animal that I am.

The next morning, Tena made breakfast. Oh my gosh, I appreciated that so much since I still don't have the energy to stand for a long time or bend over to find pots and pans.

It was a wonderful treat to enjoy a delicious breakfast, especially with a smiling friend sitting across from me!

Without applying an ice pack constantly, my left side is still swelling. It is uncomfortable to keep the ice on there, but I feel stronger.

I will be a phoenix with bad hair, but I will still rise from the ashes and get back on my feet!

April 2014

Back pain and new, sharp pain in my right shoulder are just too much to deal with. So I made an appointment with my pain management doctor.

Until lately, only the joints on my left side have been affected my arthritis. I prepared to hear the doctor say that the arthritis has now gravitated to the other side of my body.

But thank goodness, complications from breast cancer cause the pain.

Yep, the mastectomy is affecting my back. When the stinging starts from nerves and muscles trying to attach, I involuntarily jerk, which sends my back into spasms. And then inflammation sets in.

The arthritis has not traveled to the joints on the other side of my body. And that is awesome news.

Chapter Twenty-Five

For most of my life, I had to be half dead before I would finally break down and see a doctor. I just never wanted to take the time. I saw a doctor only when arthritis problems required injections or I contracted a nasty round of strep throat. Years ago my family doctor talked to me about the fact that I came to his office after working all day, with a temperature of 103. When I explained that I couldn't really be absent from my job without all kinds of make-up work piled higher than my head, he didn't seem to care.

"You have to listen to your body," he said that day. "When your body speaks, you have to listen."

I didn't bother to tell him that I couldn't really afford to listen to my body's aches and pains, that I live in the real world, where my sick days were saved to stay home with my little boy when he was under the weather. I did not heed my doctor's advice. I continued to show up only when I couldn't physically push through whatever my ailment happened to be.

Now that breast cancer has moved into my life, I find myself at the doctor's office more frequently than the grocery store. And it isn't only one doctor visit, either. That is still a tough adjustment. Right this minute, I have appointment reminders taped to the front of my fridge for doctor visits through the end of the year. Not fun.

But on the bright side, I have a wonderful comfort level with all of my doctors and the nurses, too. They have become my friends. That means so much to me, to spend these very difficult months with medical professionals who cheer me on and share about their families and lives. How can you get through the rough spots if you feel like you're just another warm body on the exam table?

May 2014

Today, I lined up with other medicine-needing people at the pharmacy.

But some lady was talking her face off to the pharmacist. In painful detail, she explained her back surgery and the prognosis. Then she jumped right into a lively tale of rehab before talking about her diabetes and her pooping problems.

I stood behind her, wanting to gag her with my damn flip flop.

I wanted to slap the pharmacist, too.

"Take control," I wanted to yell. "You aren't the therapist, okay? Get rid of her! Tell her to call Dr. Phil."

Sometimes I am entertained by the hateful stuff that crosses my mind. And sometimes I am embarrassed by those mean thoughts.

Sometimes it actually shocks me that a sudden surge of temper rushes down my spine.

My head started to hurt. My side began to ache. I was not one bit sure I could stop myself from pouncing on that lady to shut her big fat motor mouth.

On the way out, I paid at the cosmetic counter for a bottle of Pepto-Bismol and a bottled water. Since there were no customers, the clerk suggested that I exit through the "enter" door instead of walking all the way around.

I assumed she figured out that I felt like hell.

But as I planned to make my exit through the entrance, a busy-body guy appeared at the entrance and yelled at me for using the wrong door.

The employee spluttered quickly that she gave me permission.

I turned into a dragon lady and snapped at him. "Is that okay with you?"

Sometimes I hate people, especially those who think they know everything. Those who want to poke their nose in my damn business and tell me what to do.

I want people to mind their own business and shut the hell up.

And I hope that the very rude old guy gets cornered by the motor mouth lady. He deserves it.

May 2014

I've been discussing lots of topics with other women who have had breast cancer. Many times, these deep discussions take place in the middle of the night, on Facebook private messages, with other women who are also beyond exhausted but, like me, they can't sleep, either.

A few days ago, we talked about being hurt.

We are sadly amazed that we have trudged through life with such a tolerance for being treated disrespectfully.

Why didn't we demand something better?

Maybe we believed we didn't deserve better.

This isn't a subject set aside only for breast cancer survivors, though. This is a fact about many women. It just happens to be in the forefront for us right now because, for whatever reason, breast cancer has bubbled into being about so much more than boobs.

One woman's husband said she cries over nothing. That she is being a baby. She has had plenty of time to adjust. She needs to just get over it now. Move on.

This woman doesn't feel that she can forgive her husband for how he has behaved.

She doesn't feel that she can love someone who won't allow her to grieve in her own way without fear of ridicule.

She doesn't believe he could possibly love her yet treat her that way.

We talked about the fact that maybe her husband is simply afraid of her pain. He's uncomfortable with the tears. He doesn't know what to do to "fix" the situation.

But then we realized that we were making excuses for him to be an ass.

A grown-up steps in and offers comfort. A grown-up asks questions about how his wife feels and how he can help her.

My heart hurts for her. But I am relieved for myself.

I might be alone, but at least my feelings are mine. I am free, in my own environment, to go through the bad days in my own way, without feeling like I have to hide my heart or be something different just so a man won't be uncomfortable.

Sometimes I feel almost afraid of conversations like these with other deeply wounded women.

I don't like to dig up my own hurts. I don't want to face things I've already known for years but not yet been brave enough to see.

But there's an incredible power found at the core of discussions with authentic women.

Facing pain is part of growth and maturity. Facing fear is part of life, too, whether you like that or not.

All of those things were triggered when breast cancer came knocking. It tore through every facade we worked so hard to hide behind.

Lose your breasts and you somehow lose the need to bullshit yourself, too.

Breast cancer gives you the courage to not just grab hold of your life and hold on tight, but to also analyze it and think about ways to make it better.

May 2014

Today, I saw the breast surgeon.

Those wicked-ass scissors crunching through a new stitch felt like they were snipping at big chunks of my epidermis.

The best part is that my incisions continue to look better and better. That's great news, of course. But boy, my brand new boobilas still hurt.

And the evil blood pressure still isn't under control.

On a positive note, I should be strong enough in a month or so to undergo the surgery to remove my last ovary.

After that, my poor old fallopian tubes will need to look for a fun retirement community.

May 2014

Today I discovered that, because I have very little sensation on my chest, I can't feel my bathing suit top when it rides up.

I wore the top while I was cleaning house, to see how long I could wear it before the incisions are irritated.

165

When I looked in the mirror, I noticed that the left cup of the bathing suit top had moved all the way over to the center of my chest. The implant was exposed. Yet I could not feel that.

That's right. The pup without a face was playing peek-a-boo with my reflection. I might need to apply some duct tape or glue. I don't want to traumatize any beach lovers.

Chapter Twenty-Six

I am discovering that blood pressure problems really mess with my mojo. I feel light-headed and weak. Sometimes, I can't tilt my head back to wash my hair or take a long, hot shower. My head feels foggy. When that feeling comes over me, I get the hell out of there. Lord knows I don't want to fall and injure myself. I'm not too fond of the possibility of dying on the shower floor, either. With either scenario, someone would eventually find me, naked as a jaybird and boobless.

Let's just say I want to avoid that scenario at all costs.

I can't walk off the stress yet because I'm not supposed to perspire. Can't get the incisions sweaty; they might get infected. I follow the doctor's orders and try not to exert myself. And to keep from sweating, I use the window air conditioner instead of the box fan, even though air conditioning freezes me to death. When I find myself thinking about a few things in my life that cause me a lot of emotional pain, I grab a book or call a friend to laugh with about silly things that bring me no stress.

I read again about meditation. I find some examples on YouTube. I even find a meditation class in the area where I live. On my own, I try to shut everything out. I mentally picture a big broom in my head, sweeping away the worry about my parents paying my bills. I sweep away my anxieties about driving safely in the rain. I try to stop obsessing about whether the incisions are healing. I stop myself from trying to examine how I feel about being a woman with no breasts. The more I try to sweep it all away, the more often those thoughts rush right back into my brain. They even bring along new thoughts. For whatever reason, I cannot clear my head. I cannot calm down. I feel like a rubber band, stretched too tight, ready to break at any moment.

May 2014

Funny thing about breast cancer: It seems to unlock every single nook and cranny of my mind.

I guess that's not a bad thing. But I can't say that it's entirely pleasant, either. And so, last night when I couldn't sleep, I thought about the fact that I've never bought curtains. Not once. In any of my relationships.

The closest I ever came to curtains was a valance for a kitchen window.

Since the valance obviously didn't cover the window, then it didn't pass my test as a real curtain.

In my mind, you only do the curtain thing if you know that you will be making a home somewhere. But I knew I wouldn't be staying in any of my experiments with bliss.

One husband asked me a few times to buy blinds.

But I never did it.

My excuse was that I can't measure very well. That's not a lie, either.

But in the back of my mind, I think I wanted him to buy what he liked. I knew that I wouldn't be around long enough for those blinds to ever need replaced.

I didn't realize this weirdness about myself during the marriages. But in the last four years, I've grown into knowing it as a truth.

No matter how whacked it may sound, my curtain-buying phobia is still a truth. I can diagnose myself with commitment phobia sprinkled with crazy. But absolutely, I lived "survival of the fittest." There will never be a man who takes me down. Never.

My unwillingness to buy curtains was symbolic, maybe, for my unwillingness to be completely vulnerable in relationships. And my not-so-subconscious belief that every relationship ends.

I didn't give everything that I am to my relationships. Nope. I never did.

And now, I think a lot about that.

May 2014

While my surgeon snipped again today at the very tender stitches, she and her nurse commented that I don't look old enough to have a 31-year-old son. That was sweet of them, since I feel 87 years old most of the time.

"You're healing beautifully," my doctor said.

But dang it, I am still grounded from getting in the water at the beach.

She helped me to sit upright on the exam table and said, "Okay Sherri, you're done."

It took a minute to process that statement. Every Monday for weeks and weeks, I've been here. And now we are done? I'm done with breast cancer? Are you kidding me?

"Come back and see me in three months," she said with a sweet grin.

I am still restricted from lifting. But I'm free.

I started to cry. Other faces in the room were wet, too. That's what women do for each other, you know. They feel.

169

"So you're still not doing nipples?" she asked.

"Lotuses," I said.

Two of the nurses walked with me to the reception desk. "I can't believe I got here," I said to them. "I had no idea I was this close."

One nurse pulled up her scrubs to show me a couple of tats on her legs. She told me she was thinking about my plan to get lotuses instead of nipples and she had found some beautiful drawings of lotuses on Pinterest.

I was so thankful and happy that she moved past her role as nurse to share these moments.

"You've done great, Sherri," they said as I turned to leave. "Come back and see us."

My heart was doing the cha-cha as I stepped out in the sun.

I got my Pink Army badge today, the one for patience.

I can survive anything. And I will remind every woman God sends my way, that making it through breast cancer is difficult but joyful, heart-breaking but beautiful.

I will do my best to celebrate the lessons breast cancer has taught me about my life.

May 2014

The first summer I lived in Florida, I immediately understood why my sweet grandma and my great aunts joked about placing Kotex under their baking breasts. At least some of the perspiration was caught in those handy little pads of cotton.

Last summer I felt gross. Long boobs don't get much of a breeze under them, you know. They just sort of spread out all over your chest and sweat like two old lazy sows.

This summer I won't have that problem.

Here it is springtime already. Temperatures sometimes flirt with ninety degrees.

Today, I wore a very soft sports bra under a blouse.

Initially, I thought about how odd it was, not to feel breasts resting on my chest. Not to feel sweat trickling down my cleavage.

Within a few miles, the sports bra started to rub on the incisions. The incisions I happen to be guarding with my life so they can heal.

It didn't take long at all to realize that trying to wear the bra was a stupid idea.

I pulled into a McDonald's parking lot, hurried to the ladies room and yanked that thing off.

I realized that I only wore the dumb bra out of habit. Not because I had anything on my chest to put in it.

What a nice feeling, to crank the air and wear only a cotton top over the poor sore kitty heads.

I am learning as I go.

May 2014

The gynecologist ordered an ultrasound. But I didn't know, until I got to the dimly lit room, that it was a vaginal ultrasound.

Once again, I was crying. I just cannot take surprises.

I am sure that I look like the biggest baby in the world.

171

I still can't take surprises or moments when I have to be around hateful people. I absolutely fall apart. And when I fall apart, it's harder and harder to get back up again.

In the bathroom, I have myself a meltdown and manage to return to the test, with new courage.

For heaven's sake, compared to what I have already gone through, this test is a stroll through the park. I can do this. Of course I can.

After the ultrasound, I sat for an hour in the waiting room.

By the time I was led to the gynecologist's exam room, I was half sick with anxiety. I was afraid she would stare at me with big, sad eyes and say, "Well Sherri, I'm so sorry. But we found something suspicious in the ultrasound results."

But when my doctor finally appeared in the exam room, she happily informed me that Helen, my lone ovary, is shriveled. That's right, the old gal is half dead in there. And so, she isn't a threat.

I don't think I've ever been so thankful to hear that something inside my body is basically all dried up and useless.

In six months, we will evaluate the situation again. But for now, no surgery.

Thank you, God. No more surgery.

I can just focus on healing from this one.

I'm closer and closer to returning to some kind of life.

Those sweet nurses high-fived me when I happily left the exam room. They are adorable and I love them all for being my cheerleaders when I could barely hold my head up.

Cautiously, I dare to think it's over now ... until June when I see the oncologist for my six-month check-up.

Until August, when I see the plastic surgeon again to check the implants and incisions.

It's a brief glimpse ... maybe three weeks ... but I will take these brief little moments to dance around with some freedom bubbling in my throat.

It makes me crazy happy that I have some breathing room between doctor visits.

Because of this, I can do more with my time than try to remember which office I'm supposed to visit and what time I need to be there.

May 2014

Damn it.

Almost 1:45 a.m. For the last 40 minutes, the right side of my chest has throbbed along with intermittent, stabbing pains that take my breath.

I have to talk to myself ... talk myself off the ledge.

"No, the implant has not ruptured. You just saw the doctor a few days ago. Everything looked great!"

"You've had this type of pain plenty of other times. It's very likely the nerves trying again to reconnect. Just take your medicine and go back to bed."

So I took the pain pill that hurts my stomach. Maybe the focus will switch from the squealing fake boob and go directly to nausea.

Earlier this evening, I felt just fine. But wham ... now my chest is on fire.

I am more than tired of these feel-like-hell moments.

But I am tough. I can take this. I am so close to the end of this.

If I end up crying again, that's okay.

It doesn't mean I'm not strong. It only reminds me that I am tired.

Hopefully, God will shine down on me and say, "Nice job. You have shown me that you can hang with the toughest times."

Chapter Twenty-Seven

At my last appointment with the breast surgeon, I asked how long I had to wait before I could get back in the water. She said to wait two more weeks. I wanted very much to return to my mermaid ways. But I was afraid. Instead of waiting two weeks, I waited nearly a month. Just to be on the safe side.

Every day, I inspected the incisions with a hand mirror to make sure nothing had broken open. I was afraid of infection. I was afraid of so many things that I never used to even think about. It made me mad at myself.

Before breast cancer, I was the fearless one. The goofball who would do anything on a dare. But now I was different. Tightly wound with a big thick streak of catastrophic thought screaming through the middle of my brain. I was afraid I was turning into the kind of person who fears every little something.

I have never lived my life by fearing anything except emotional pain. I have always been a free spirit. I have always loved anything unpredictable and everything that took my breath. I didn't want to be this person who clenched her fists and held her breath. I didn't want to be so afraid of so many things. But I was. And I couldn't seem to grab hold of my courage. Most of the time, I couldn't even *find* my damn courage. I was still terrified to drive in the rain. Still couldn't sleep in my bed.

And now I delayed getting in the water.

For as long as I can remember, I've been in love with the beach. It is a salve for me. It is the place where I find peace and clarity. I have made every major life decision while floating on a raft in that water. I was realizing though, that I was now taking that away from myself, too. Out of fear.

I sat on the sand with my friends and laughed when one of them pointed out that my bathing suit top was again traveling past an implant. I walked into the water with them but never too far, never higher than my thighs. I didn't want to take a chance on a wave crashing across my chest.

The day I finally took that first dip in the Gulf of Mexico was heaven. It was a spontaneous decision, like so many others in my life. It felt like my spirit rushed up behind my fear, shoved it out of the way and threw me back into who I used to be. In that moment, as the warm June water rushed over my hair and my chest, I was so thankful. I felt so free. Once again, I made it to the other side of fear. I stepped through another moment with the me I used to be.

I treasured that feeling. It reminded me that the core of who I really am was still there, still trying to stand up. And that's all I needed to know. I could keep trying to climb across the anxiety just as long as I could remind myself that breast cancer had only taken my breasts, not my soul.

June 2014

Earlier in the week, my blood pressure medication was changed for the third time. But I still suffered with vertigo, the most debilitating experience I've ever had. On one of those vertigo days, I could not sit up without puking.

The room spun.

I was supposed to meet my friend Ronnie for lunch. And later in the day, I planned to meet another friend for an art event. I managed to text Ronnie and ask her to please bring me some Sprite or ginger ale.

I hated for her to drive so far out of her way. I hated to need her help so badly, But thank goodness she came to the beach with Sprite in tow.

She wanted me to go to the hospital. But I felt like I just needed a couple of days to adjust to the new medication. Then I would be alright.

Bless her heart, every time I had to puke, I asked Ronnie to go out on the porch. I was embarrassed to throw up in front of her. The temperature on the back porch was probably anything but comfortable for her, but she did it.

Also, lucky for me, her OCD tendencies kicked in and she cleaned out my fridge and practically alphabetized my food. At the time, I didn't notice that she was doing all of that since I could barely open my eyes without throwing up. A day later, when I opened the fridge and saw that the cleaning fairy had been busy in there, it made me laugh. She's such a sweetie. She and Elaine do everything they can to get me organized. But I'm a human tornado, a walking mess. I am so grateful that they love me anyway.

But this was another example of fighting with reality. Once again, I refused to accept how sick I felt.

I continued to believe that I would miraculously get past the vertigo, hop in the shower, wear my new dress and meet my other friend later in the afternoon.

Two hours before I was set to meet her, I had to struggle to sit up long enough to send my friend a text that I couldn't be there.

All night, I entertained myself with morbid thoughts about dying on my couch with my face in the trash can. I couldn't stand up, couldn't open my eyes.

I was embarrassed that I couldn't be at my friend's event. I was mad at myself for again for being willing to simple face the fact that I could not possibly go.

My friend was hurt and angry with me. Because I texted her so late in the day, she didn't have time to make a new plan. She was also mad because I texted her instead of calling.

Rather than fighting for the friendship, I let it go. I completely understood her feelings. But I could not give to her what I did not have. The truth was that I could barely sift through my fears about the blood pressure issues. I was afraid of the fact that it continued to spike so dangerously. I didn't understand why I could not tolerate the medications to get it under control.

Simply put, I could not be the kind of friend she needed.

And I did not have the energy to explain to her how my life had been turned all the way around by breast cancer and fear and high blood pressure, vertigo, anxiety.

Sometimes there aren't words to explain to someone else that you're trying as hard as you can. And even though I was so sorry that I had to cancel, I was trying as hard as I could to stay sane.

Obviously, it was not enough to keep that friendship from wilting.

I had nothing else to give to her. Nothing but an apology.

Chapter Twenty-Eight

A week or so after that lengthy party with vertigo and puke buckets, I felt even more awful. Every few minutes, I found myself drenched with sweat. I was so weak that I was shaky. I was trying to work. But far too often, I had to put my head on the table and get myself together.

When I still didn't feel better by late afternoon, I took my blood pressure. I can't remember the reading now, but I do remember thinking that my blood pressure cuff must be malfunctioning. If this reading was correct, shouldn't I be dead?

I didn't want the big fuss of calling 911. Absolutely, I wanted to avoid the big drama of fire trucks squealing into my neighborhood. So I drove myself the two or three miles, very slowly, to the fire department. With sweat dripping through my hair, I sat in a chair while the firefighters stared down at me. All I wanted was to get my blood pressure with their cuff so I could compare the readings. But I was suddenly being interrogated. One of the men asked health history questions. I found it difficult to say that I underwent a third surgery six weeks ago for breast cancer.

Sometimes those words still don't feel like they should be part of who I am.

Sometimes I still have to shove that sentence off my tongue because my ears still don't like to hear it. But while I explained the reasons for three surgeries in five months and the stress I was under, which spiked my vitals, fear climbed up my back. Maybe something really was wrong with me. But I kept it to myself and waited for the results with their blood pressure cuff. Hmm. Nothing was wrong with my apparatus.

Their reading was like mine.

Very low.

Dangerously low.

Even though I explained that I was now adjusting to my third prescription for blood pressure, I found myself in an ambulance, en route to the emergency room. So dizzy I couldn't open my eyes, I didn't feel exactly afraid. More than anything, I felt exhausted. I was tired of everything related to breast cancer and the stress it brought to my life. I felt beat up by it all. That was my first experience riding in an ambulance as a patient. It might have been at least a little bit entertaining if I hadn't felt like death.

Once in the emergency room, I was whisked into a small exam room with one male EMT, two male techs and a female nurse. When I was moved from the stretcher to the bed, one of the techs grabbed the bottom of my dress and yanked it up, trying to remove it. This action horrified me.

Under the dress, I was wearing nothing but panties. I can't even describe the panic that shot through me. Other than female friends, no one has seen my chest except for my doctor, my nurses and me. To say that I felt humiliated is a gross understatement.

"Stop it," I said as I grabbed his hands. "I've had a mastectomy. And you're not taking off my dress."

He very impatiently reminded me that they needed to quickly do tests and find out what was going on with me. But I had a death grip on his hands. In that moment, I would rather die than allow that ass to remove my dress and humiliate me. I glared at him, feeling absolute rage that he would treat me or any woman with such disrespect. There was no way I would let go of his hands or the fabric of my dress. And it didn't take long for him to figure that out.

"I will change into the gown on my own," I said in a shaky but firm voice. I was trying not to cry all over the place. I was embarrassed. I also wanted to slap the holy shit out of him. I was prepared to unleash seven months of breast cancer hell on his hind end. Finally, he let go and they all turned their heads.

Privately, I changed from my dress to the stupid hospital gown, still so angry about the incident that I was shaking. They shouldn't treat people like blobs of nothing. They shouldn't have a female patient in an exam room with more males than females. Even if I still had breasts, that scenario would have bothered me.

I was disturbed too by the feelings that rolled around inside of me when I realized the tech might expose my chest to everyone in the room. It was a feeling much like a deep, unsettled shame, which made me mad at myself. Obviously, it was not my fault that I lost my breasts. Where did that hot jolt of shame come from?

I would have wrestled that guy to the floor to prevent anyone from seeing my scarred up chest. And that feeling, that protective, beat-up, helpless feeling, put permanent tears in my eyes.

Unexplainable bouts with vertigo, coupled with the fact that breast cancer sometimes travels to the brain, resulted in a CAT scan. It was the longest hour or so of my life, fearing that the ER doctor would waltz in and announce that some questionable spots were found on my brain. I have known people with brain cancer. I know that brain cancer nearly always leads to a messy death. And I wasn't ready to check out, not after all I had already been through.

During the test, I kept my eyes squeezed shut while tears dripped down both sides of my neck. I promised God that I would work harder at getting myself more centered and less stressed. I promised that I would do whatever was necessary to lighten the load on my heart if He could please, please make the tests normal. It was a very frightening experience. Knowing there was even a remote possibility that breast cancer had traveled to a new area of my body put my heart on high alert.

After the test, I was returned to the little exam room. Grateful

181

to be alone, I stared at the ceiling, barely remembering to breathe. I was scared to death. If the doctor popped his head around that curtain and said, "I'm sorry but the tests show masses ..." I had no idea how I would hold onto my mind. Fear settled into nausea. I covered my face with my hand, starting taking deep breaths to calm down and stopped worrying about the fact that my tears were flying all over the place.

"There is nothing you can do about any of this," I whispered under my breath. "So just breathe. You can handle whatever happens. Even if you hear that you're dying, you will be strong."

At 11:30 that evening, the emergency room doctor finally appeared in the doorway. The moment I saw him, I immediately felt vomit in my throat. The last time I was terrified enough to puke, I was heading toward the first surgery. Now here I was a second time, scared enough to barf all over the place. I stared at him, trying to read his face. Very calmly, he announced that the scan was clear. That I needed to stop taking the blood pressure medications for now and follow up on Monday with my family doctor.

I just nodded. But when the doctor left the room, I dropped my head and whispered a thank you to God. I had a cancer-free body. I absolutely would not lose sight again of the fact that I had to take care of myself. Very literally, I had to take care of myself. I had me and that's all I had. I needed to remember that. And I needed to get a lot more serious about giving myself what I needed. If I didn't get busy deciding that I mattered, I might not be in the world a lot longer.

I privately traded the hospital gown for my comfortable yet butt-ugly gauze tent dress. Then I called a cab and stood alone outside the emergency room doors in the sticky night air. It was a shaky and sad feeling to stand there, waiting for a taxi to pull up to the curb. Plenty of times in my life, I have felt alone. But that experience, waiting for the test results alone then standing outside the hospital alone? Definitely in the top five of being kicked in the heart with the reminder that I'm traveling through life as a solo act. I knew I could call one of my friends or a cousin. But why in the world would I get anybody out this late at night, to drive me eight miles? That would have been rude, not to mention unnecessary.

Later, I realized that it was probably good for me to go through that whole scary block of time alone. On one hand, I was once again reminded that when all the chips appear to be down, I am strong. I can get through things on my own. But on the other hand, that Lone Ranger experience reminded me that because of who I've been for 54 years, because of my trust issues, my stubbornness and my ridiculous need to feel independent, because of all those pieces of me, I was alone in moments when I desperately wished I wasn't.

When I think back on that June evening, my heart fills up with an awkward mix of my rather bitter reality mixed with my losses and a few of those old dreams I never talk about anymore.

June 2014

My family doctor pointed out that I absolutely must get rid of any stresses in my life. My body is too weak to take on these extra burdens. In fact, the blood pressure problem is the very tangible sign that I cannot afford to be upset.

Not by anyone.

Not about anything.

I got busy doing nothing. And a few days later, I was back in the doctor's office to get a new reading.

Thankfully, my blood pressure had come down on its own.

I got another lecture about how stress obviously affects me.

It's the same lecture I received a few weeks earlier at the breast surgeon's office.

I don't tell either doctor that the message has no clear answer. I don't know how to unload all that I am carrying around on my heart. But I will keep trying.

June 2014

Since my little trip to the emergency room, I sometimes think about the red-hot panic that rose in my throat.

I can't get away from it. I can't un-feel what I experienced emotionally when I realized that the rude tech was trying to take my dress off of me.

Because I reacted that way, does it mean that I am shallow?

Somewhere in my deepest thoughts, do I actually think I'm no longer a "real" woman since I have no breasts?

Sometimes I still cry about my chest.

I don't care who thinks I should "get over it."

I really don't care.

If they are somehow bothered by the fact that I sometimes cry about my lost breasts, then they should stay away from me.

A couple of people in my life have said, "Sherri, why do you say you don't have breasts anymore? Yes you do. You have perky new boobs now. Why are you making such a big deal of this?"

I always scream in my head, "You don't know one damn thing about what you're saying. I lost my breasts, you idiot. These are implants. They don't feel like breasts. They don't look like breasts. They don't have nipples on them, either. Stop saying I have new boobs. Just shut up."

A lot of the time, the people who make those dumb-ass remarks try to appear to rally on my account, try to convince me that what I feel is not really true.

But actually, when it gets down to the truth, the people who make those remarks don't want to deal with my pain. They don't want to see it, hear it, feel it.

Maybe they think that during a weak moment I will just suddenly perk up and say, "Wow! You're right! Why didn't I notice before that I actually like these things a whole lot better than I ever liked having breasts? Silly me!"

The truth is that I always try to look for the good stuff. And there are definite perks to having implants. Some mastectomy patients can't get implants at all.

Plus, I no longer need underwire bras and underwire bathing suit tops.

I am only one of millions of women with mastectomy who would immediately take back my saggy old Tiff and Alex if that was a choice.

But it's not.

I also get sick of hearing, "Well at least you are cancer free!"

I press my lips together during those moments too, so I can stop myself from yelling, "I know that! I know it, okay? Of course I am thankful to be cancer-free, you weirdo! Who wouldn't be? But being cancer-free cost me my breasts. And I am still grieving them ... just as you would grieve. So stop suggesting that I can't grieve the breasts I had for more than 40 years. Stop suggesting that I am somehow not grateful enough to have survived cancer just because I miss having my own breasts."

June 2014

Sometimes I feel like an imposter, walking around in public, giving the illusion that under my clothes, I look like any other woman.

Under my clothes, I have a war zone. A battle was fought on my chest.

I am not a "regular" woman anymore.

Every now and then I think about romantic moments with a particular husband who absolutely adored my breasts. I teased him with my huge knockers. Rubbed them on his face while he laughed and pretended to smother.

But I can't imagine straddling a husband, leaning forward and having nothing on my chest anymore except these odd little skin pockets.

I would not want to press my naked chest against a man's. His fingers would touch jagged scars, not the soft flesh of a normal female breast. His hands could search forever in the darkness and never find nipples.

What happened in the emergency room was a knee-jerk response. And it came from a deep place of fear and shame and embarrassment.

I wish I didn't have to know this about myself.

I wish I could go on believing that I am adjusting like a trouper ...

Unfortunately though, I do know that frantic feeling that roared through my chest as I grabbed that male tech's hands.

Sometimes, I wonder if one of my biggest fears is that my chest would be exposed to a man ... a man who can't drop his gaze before I see disgust in his eyes.

Chapter Twenty-Nine

Still worrying about the high blood pressure, I start to think I need someone to talk to. Someone who doesn't know me. Someone who will talk seriously and honestly with me about how I am feeling and what I fear.

Some of the things that eat away at my heart are very private. I don't feel comfortable about discussing them with anyone else. Chances are good that I won't share those secrets with a therapist, either. But I make an appointment anyway. I am starting to think that the blood pressure problem is possibly related to depression.

At the first appointment, I decide that the very soft-spoken female therapist is probably one of the coolest people I have ever met. Her office is dotted with all kinds of unusual keepsakes, from odd-looking rocks to runaway plants, pillows and stools in fun Bohemian prints and two couches that are so comfortable, I just want to stretch out for a nap on one of them.

I feel uncomfortable when I notice her watching my leg shake nervously, up and down, fifty miles a minute. I feel uncomfortable when she asks me to tell her about myself. My face just about burns off because I don't want to say that I've been married and divorced three times. I don't want to say that I am afraid that I can't find a job I can physically do, now that my back is rotten and my breasts have been chopped off.

I don't want to confess that I am more afraid of filing for disability than I am about finding a job that I can physically do. I don't want to say that I view disability as giving in and surrendering. She might not understand that. She might think I am being stubborn for no reason. And then I will hate her cool guts for judging me and I won't ever want to come back here to envy all of her cool little knickknacks.

She asks me how I feel about the breast cancer and I truly think I mean it when I say that I have adjusted to what I have been through. Then we talk about my blood pressure. She starts to teach me some relaxation techniques. And then she tells me to take in a deep breath, hold my breath and cross my arms over my chest. I think we are continuing with relaxation tips. So I feel kicked in the gut when, out of the blue, the therapist says, "Tell me how it feels to put your arms across your chest and not feel your breasts there anymore."

Well, I probably don't need to even tell you what happened the moment that sentence left her mouth. My heart fell out of my chest and rolled under the Persian rug while the rest of me exploded in a big nasty mess of tears and pain.

"Tell me all the reasons why you are crying right now," she said.

And I was rather shocked at myself that every single one of my deepest hurts flew out of my mouth. One after another. Every hurt. Every worry. Everything that weighed me down hurled itself out of my chest. I kept my head down, not entirely convinced that if I looked up, I wouldn't see all of that pain littering the cool office. Jagged black pieces of deep, deep hurt and worries, stress, lies, betrayal, exhaustion and tension.

I returned a couple more times to the counselor's office and then I stopped. One reason I stopped had to do with money. But another reason was that I felt like I got everything from her that I needed, which was a safe place to talk about the raw core of my pain. Once I realized that yes, I could survive, I didn't feel a need to see the therapist anymore.

Chapter Thirty

Lots of people avoid visiting the Florida beaches during July and August. They can't handle the merciless Florida heat and that intense sun, so hot on the sand that your bare feet sizzle.

But I'm not one of those people.

I have always wished that I could be one of those awesome, put-together women who wears a cute ponytail, jewelry and a pretty cover-up to the beach. Plenty of times, I have watched these types of women stroll past in a whiff of perfume while the sun glints on their bracelets and earrings.

I might wish for that shit, but I sure can't seem to be that woman.

I don't wear jewelry to the beach. I think that's stupid. I don't wear make-up, either, for the same reason. And most of the time, I go to the beach with bedhead. My cover-up idea is a 15-year-old tank top. And I smell like a sweat ball, not a sweet little bouquet of fresh flowers.

No matter how scuzzy I look when I'm there, I happen to love the hot sand and the power of the sun. I love the warm gulf waters. I love that tourists take cover in the middle of the summer and stay in their own hometowns.

I am absolutely in love with the fact that nearly every afternoon, a summer thunder storm rolls in.

It's like Christmas to me, except it's every single day.

I am still in awe of lightning flashing across the sky and thunder, rolling so forcefully that it vibrates in my chest. Every single time it storms, I happily take my favorite seat on the porch to write and enjoy the scent and sound of rain.

When I found this little beach house, it was a big mess, in the midst of being remodeled. Previous renters had not loved it at all the way that I love it now.

The moment I saw it, I was in love. I could see past how trashed it was on the inside. Old lady trees bow over the back porch by the canal. Egrets stroll along the seawall like royalty. Mullets dive-bomb from one splash in the murky water to another. Squirrels skitter around in the trees, playing in the coolness of early morning. And the lizards! Well they are everywhere, and I just love those little guys, too.

But the most important reason I wanted to be here so badly had everything to do with my love for rain and the sound it makes on the roof of this little cottage.

I can't think of much else that makes me feel more cozy and happy than to listen to the rain. Sometimes it pounds so hard that I can't hear my phone ring. But I love it anyway. This experience does something so happy to my heart. It does something so peaceful to my whole life. Every time the rain comes, it feels like the first time I fell in love with it.

I am very grateful that I went through breast cancer right here, surrounded by the beach and the sun, the mellow people, the awesome storms. After so many years of perching in so many places, either in bad relationships or in rental properties I loathed, I finally have a place I dearly love to be. During these very trying months, the reminder to myself that I have a place to be — a place that speaks to my heart — well, it has brought me through some very difficult moments. Each time I left a doctor's appointment, my body felt like a yawn as soon as I crossed the island bridge.

For all of my life, I have hoped for a place to truly nest. I was always envious of my friends as they searched for something special for a fireplace mantel or a hallway or a space above their bed. I never understood that feeling since I never loved anywhere I ever landed. And beside that fact, I always knew I wouldn't be staying there forever anyway.

All of my life, I wished to purchase a home of my own. But I never made enough money. I was afraid of the surprise maintenance needs of home ownership, such as digging a new water line or replacing a roof. It's safe to say that I won't ever be able to afford to purchase this little cracker box. I won't bask in that feeling of truly knowing that this little cottage is mine, that no one can take it away from me. But I can certainly try to focus on today. I can fall in love with this little house, over and over again. I can enjoy it for as long as I am allowed by the landlord to be here.

As the temperature dropped last winter, it suddenly dawned on me that I never saw a furnace. And sure enough, after some brief investigation, I realized that my little beach nest has no heat. So I bought a couple of space heaters. I closed off both bedrooms and blasted the heaters toward the couch, which was piled high with blankets. Some nights were miserably cold — but never bad enough for me to leave.

Sometimes I lose power here, and that's one reason a monster flashlight graces every room. I happen to hate the dark. Then one night, I blew a breaker by trying to use a third space heater. While cold rain and wind whipped my hair around my face and drenched my pajamas, I was outside with my flashlight, dealing with the breaker box and sobbing my head off.

Sure it was a miserable moment. But again, it was never a bad enough moment to make me abandon ship. This little cottage, which isn't even 800 square feet, is definitely where my heart loves to beat.

July 2014

I've turned into some kind of boob captain. I just can't keep my nose out of other women's boob business.

When I enter conversations with other women, I always manage to work in the question, "Are you consistently getting your mammogram each year?"

For a while, I carried around the phone number for the traveling pink van that provides low-cost mammograms for women with no insurance. And sometimes I am surprised that so many women seem to blow off the importance of self-breast exams followed by annual mammograms.

Still, women write to me on Facebook or get my phone number from other women who know me.

Some of the women admit that they are afraid to schedule a mammogram since they haven't had one in several years.

Others have no health insurance.

And some call with fear in their voices. Their mammogram has to be repeated or breast biopsies are scheduled. Their stories put a lump in my throat.

Chapter Thirty-One

One of my friends hates for me to refer to my serial divorces as "failed marriages." She always says that if I learned anything from those experiences, then they were not at all failures.

Personally, I think that is a bit of a stretch.

The truth is that I did fail. And obviously, I didn't learn what I should have learned or I wouldn't have failed over and over again.

My happily-married-forevers legally lasted an average of five years, if that.

In retrospect, the wheels fell off the wagon within the first year or two. But for some reason, I continued to push that dilapidated wagon — up hill, with no wheels and no traction — hoping that if I could get it to the top, it wouldn't rush off the other side of the mountain without me.

But it always did.

Once you've been married and divorced multiple times, you are socially marked forever. You are damaged goods, especially if you are female. If regular people say it's not true, just ask a woman with a few divorces under her belt. She will tell you that it is painfully difficult to admit to so many failures. It is gut-wrenching to know that even if you can conjure up a bit of self-esteem and attract a more well-rounded man, "nice" guys will run in the opposite direction when they hear about a woman with a bunch of divorces in her history.

Who wants to introduce a retired serial wife to their very nice, wholesome families?

No one.

That's the true answer.

It's entertaining to me sometimes when I think about possibly meeting a man who has been divorced as many times as I have. It's an embarrassing double standard. But I know that I would immediately do the full body scan. My burning question would be, "What in the hell is wrong with this guy? Obviously, he's got some weirdo problems or he wouldn't be flying in and out of divorce court."

Then I would need to look at myself, of course, and realize that, no matter how hurt I might be about it, anyone who would show interest in me would immediately do the full scan in my direction, too. I would see that question in his eyes: "Hmm, what's wrong with her? Is she crazy? Is she a drunk? A drug addict? Why has this woman been divorced three times?"

I would very nicely say, "I have the self-esteem of a toaster. That's the root of all the problems in my life. I wouldn't blame you — not a bit — if you just keep moving."

Chapter Thirty-Two

Until breast cancer arrived in my life, I didn't think that much of anything could stomp me into submission. But then, I never considered dying on a surgery table. I never thought, "What if I'm on my way out?"

It feels like cancer removed my breasts and cracked my chest open so that all these parts of me were scattered all over the place. I am willing now to look at my character defects. I am willing to analyze those rough edges and make peace with them where I can. Breast cancer has also swirled new dreams around in my chest and brought me new hope and a new understanding of what I want from my life.

I have so much to be grateful for.

The truth is that breast cancer has turned out to be one of the biggest blessings in my life.

August 2014

I saw the breast surgeon today for my three-month check-up.

She says everything looks great. Healing is going well.

I told her about the "sloshing" feeling when I move. It's still uncomfortable to bend over. My chest is still stinging. It's been four months since the last surgery; why am I still dealing with this stuff?

She tells me that women who were big busted like me have a longer, harder recovery. During the mastectomy, the surgeon cuts farther under the arms and lower on the chest to make sure all the breast tissue is removed. So more muscles are cut. More nerves are damaged.

A full year of recovery is necessary for a mastectomy. And recovery from implants can take up to two years.

What the hell?

By the time I got to my car, I was crying. Like that will help anything.

It will be okay. I will make it okay. I will focus on the positive.

August 2014

Today is my sweet son's 32nd birthday. And I would give anything to kiss and hug him and tell him how much I love him. I miss him terribly. My skin hurts when I think about it.

More than once today, I have cried myself a little river.

It has been nearly a year since I have seen my only child.

Maybe I was wrong by asking my son to wait a while instead of coming to Florida to visit.

Maybe I should have allowed him to see me walking around like a 96-year-old jumbo shrimp.

After all the years of showing up for him, being invincible for him, fighting all kinds of battles for his future, I wasn't ready for him to know that my Super Mama facade is nonexistent.

But I see now that I underestimated my son's strength. I handled breast cancer with him as if he was still my little boy, not the well-educated and intelligent man that he is today.

I hope I have not hurt him by stalling. I wanted only to protect him from the first time in our lives together when he and I both privately wondered if breast cancer might force an early goodbye to each other.

And so, I spent his birthday looking at old pictures. Remembering how his beautiful little hand curled around strands of my long hair when I rocked him to sleep. Remembering how he reached for me when he was afraid, believing that the safest place to be was in my arms.

I closed my eyes and smiled, to see old visions of my sweet son ringing a bell during a preschool program, waving goodbye to me on his first day of school, honking the horn as he left the driveway to proudly drive alone for the first time.

As those precious old movies played in my head, I relived the day I drove him to college. Who knows how I managed to kiss him goodbye and not shed one tear in front of him. He never knew, of course, that I had to pull the car over on the way home. I couldn't see to drive. The tears were blinding.

Even before I met the young woman who would become my son's life partner, I knew he loved her. I knew this because I had never seen that look in my son's eyes. When her name left his lips, his eyes filled with this amazingly beautiful tenderness. That look was in his eyes again on their wedding day. And I thank God often that my son is blessed with a healthy, nurturing, forever kind of love.

I have been blessed to spend the last 32 years of my life with this ambitious, worldly young man.

His sharp wit keeps me laughing. His belief system and moral code are beautifully etched on his heart. His love for his wife is a gift for me to see. He is a good man. A devoted, loyal man.

I am more grateful than I could ever say for the son God shares with me.

Breast cancer didn't need to remind me of my love for my child

197

since he is always on my heart.

But it has reminded me that I'm nowhere close to being ready to leave my son. I'm not ready to miss so many of his tomorrows.

I am grateful every day, not to be fighting for my life.

Chapter Thirty-Three

I've run across maybe a handful of women in my life who have few, if any, female friends. Most of these women say that evil people with vaginas gossip and plot behind your back to take your man. Yes, these woman-hating females believe that being friends with males is a lot less of a hassle.

Hmm.

When I am in the company of a woman with that opinion, I think about saying that narrow-minded humans of both sexes can be catty and gossipy. I think about saying that a "friend" who can take your man is certainly not your friend. And a good man cannot be forced into cheating, anyway.

But I rarely waste my breath.

By this age, if a woman doesn't know that female friendships are worth more than gold, she's way past any help I could ever offer. After all, life is magical when you laugh with and spill your guts to a group of trusted girlfriends. Some of my best moments have been spent with dear friends.

I discovered this treasure as a child. It was such a wonderful, safe feeling to know that my friend Sheri would invite me to her birthday party and my friend Vicki would sit with me at the lunch table. In middle school and high school, my friends gathered around to share their lives with me.

I learned the soulful depth of female friendship and the spiritual connection among women when I was in my early twenties, alone with my child. Without meeting other single moms, those years would have been much more lonely. Other young women my age were living completely different lives. They were finishing college degrees, beginning careers, shopping every Saturday, dating and planning trips. But that wasn't my life at that age. I had a baby. And so, I was often socially isolated. I had nothing in common with young women who weren't also mothers. And Lord knows I was often too exhausted to do anything fun anyway, even if an opportunity came around.

When I was at the park one day with my son, I ran into an old friend from high school. She was also alone. And her child, a boy, was only six months younger than mine. We grabbed each other and hugged, knowing that finally, we both had a friend. And not just any friend, either. A friend with a baby. A friend who truly understood what it was like to be so young but so old, all at the same time.

As we talked, we realized that we worked within a few miles of each other. We both had to be on the road before 6:30 every morning. So to save gasoline, we started sharing rides every weekday to our jobs in Indianapolis. As we made that 45-minute commute, long before the sun rose in the sky on many mornings, we shared our dreams and worries. We surprised each other with snacks. We laughed a lot.

Having another single mother my age to talk to about fears and hurts meant so much. We loved our boys with all of our hearts. Occasionally, we spent time together on weekends, enjoying our children and resting from very long work weeks. A couple of times, on snow-covered roads, the car slid into a ditch on the way to work. We managed to laugh, even though we were both frozen, waiting patiently in the bitter cold as a trucker or two came to our rescue.

Another time, one of the back tires on her car went flat. It was unbelievably hot that afternoon as we walked, at least a mile along the interstate, then down the busy Washington Street ramp, to find a pay phone. As sweat poured off both of us, we laughed hysterically. My friend had forgotten to put the jack in the trunk, even though her dad reminded her several times. She swore she would not call her dad for help. She didn't want to hear a lecture several times for several months. By the time we walked all that way and found a pay phone, the decision was made. My friend would call one of her brothers' friends. Hopefully, the guy would take pity on us and rescue us before we both died from heat stroke. But my additional worry was to pick up my son before 8 p.m. at daycare or I would be charged a dollar for every minute that I was late.

She and I constantly drummed up new money-making opportunities. One of those ideas was to crawl into the Dumpsters behind a couple of frat houses on the college campus, intending to collect all the beer cans from weekend parties. We would sell the aluminum and save the money. By the time we accumulated enough cash from this little business venture, our boys would be old enough for us to take them on a fun vacation, maybe to Holiday World.

I will never forget the first Saturday morning we decided to officially do the Dumpster dive. With the boys safely belted into their car seats in my car, I wove my fingers together to make a step. Using my open palms to boost herself higher, my friend, who was shorter than me, crawled inside a Dumpster. Immediately, she started to fling beer cans. They landed in all directions on the asphalt as I chased them with an open trash bag. With the car door open, both of our little boys giggled. I couldn't blame them for laughing at the silly scene involving their mommies.

But then my friend started to cuss her brains out. From inside the Dumpster, where I could barely see the top of her head, she screamed that hundreds of honey bees were swarming around her. The louder she cussed, the faster the beer cans flew over the side of the Dumpster and the harder I laughed. A few minutes later, some of those bees picked me as their next victim. Quickly, I shut the car door so the bees wouldn't get in there with the kids. But my friend and I both ended up with stings. We laughed like crazy that day. And for weeks after that, we broke out in hysterics every time we thought about it. Eventually, we abandoned our business plan. Bee stings just weren't worth maybe $4 worth of aluminum cans.

In those first few years of motherhood, I was invited into an entire subculture of extremely strong, resilient women who were exactly like my friend from high school. For comic relief, we laughed at things that married women would never find funny. We called our exes the worst bad names we could think of for not paying child support so we could breathe a little bit easier. We were sometimes crude and rowdy. We cussed like sailors. And we cried easily — because when you're a single mother, your pain is always right there, ready to seep from your skin.

Single moms learn early that we will probably never enjoy most of what a lot of wives take for granted, such as big homes and garden tubs, enough money to get highlights and a haircut and enough time to watch a program on TV. We were envious of their cloth napkins and pretty holiday trimmings with a husband carving the expensive turkey at the head of the table. Just to deal with the hurts of not having anything even remotely like what wives could have, we made fun of it all.

On Christmas Eve, we shed more than a few tears during telephone conversations. Only single parents know how lonely it can be not to be loved by a man on Christmas Eve, and every other night too, to have someone to snuggle with when the kids are in bed. For Valentine's Day, we sometimes wrote each other funny, fake love letters from nonexistent boyfriends.

There is no doubt in my mind: Those women saved my life. Over and over again, when I found myself in the midst of unbelievable stress and hurt and disappointment, they held on tight to me. We reminded each other that we were amazing, loving mothers. That it might be a bad day or a bad week, but our children were always the prize when the storms passed. I loved those women like sisters. I still do. Through the years, some of them have passed away. But they stay on my heart forever.

The older women in that group taught me how to fight back in the middle of the good-old-boy network. They taught me to find my voice as a young mother, as a young woman. Sometimes I surprised myself with how strong I could actually be. We often shared stories that started out with hurt and ended with laughter. Sometimes the stories were about lazy exes or their snooty new wives, family members who hurt our feelings, bosses who talked to us like dirt. No matter what, those conversations ended in laughter. And because of that, we healed each other, time after time.

We also got involved with petitions through the National Organization for Women to demand that fathers either pay the child support they owed or face strong consequences. In those days, a deadbeat dad could announce to the court that he was "making an effort." And that would be that.

Of course, single mothers were enraged by those interactions. After all, none of us could go to the grocery store, the childcare center or the doctor's office and flippantly announce that we were "making an effort." We were expected to pay for those services. We were irate that so many dads skated by with no fear of consequences. Many of us watched the fathers of our children jump right back into life without the slightest bump in the road. They were not working two jobs to make ends meet. They were not explaining to disappointed little people that maybe the other parent would stop by next week or show up next time for the soccer game. Nope. So many of those fathers spent their money and their time on new girlfriends instead of their own children. It was always the exhausted mommies who healed the hearts of confused and hurt offspring. It was always the incredibly strong single moms who kept the world revolving for their children.

But when everything seemed to crumble on top of our heads, we fought back in the only way we knew how: We laughed so we could stay sane.

We laughed about the silliest things. We laughed about the most heartbreaking things.

And we never pointed out to each other that our laughter led to tears streaming down our faces.

We quietly understood and respected each other's stress and pain.

Thirty years later, I still believe that some of the most amazing people I've ever known in my life are single mothers who did it all. Day after day. Because they loved their babies as much as I loved mine.

That's one of the reasons I love to write contemporary fiction. I never water my books down. I write about women and situations and hurts that are real. I write about moments in the lives of many women I have known through the years. My characters are always strong and resourceful. They do the nasty vengeful things to men that we always fantasized about doing.

My books have always drawn amazing women to my life. Real women appreciate raw honesty. They understand and appreciate the humor and the messages found on my pages. And that means so much to me.

Breast cancer brought the same beautiful gifts: a huge new circle of fierce, amazing women.

Chapter Thirty-Four

Even though I don't want to stress myself out about it, I am realizing a few painful things.

Because of my history with divorce, I have no financial cushion. I do not own a home. I have a little tiny nest egg for retirement, and it probably wouldn't last a full year. I don't think I will ever be able to retire. Unless I develop a taste for cat food, since I wouldn't be able to afford groceries, I will have to work until the day I croak.

I look around at many women my age who did things differently. Women who have been in 30- and 40-year marriages look at retirement homes with their husbands and plan extravagant vacations. But that is not my life. I know many other women in the same boat I am in — the boat of divorced women that is taking on water. That boat.

I have fluttered around in life, from one marriage to another. From one job to another. I have lived alone for most of my adult life, and I've never made a bunch of money, even though I have worked like a dog. My financial future is pretty damn bleak. But then I know a few women who are in much more trouble than me. They bought into the Ward and June Cleaver mentality, stayed home and raised their children. And many of those women faced the shock of their lives when their fifty-ish husbands suddenly announced that they no longer wanted to be married. And so those women, middle-aged and terrified about their future with no job skills, need a lot more than I do.

It is happening more and more. There's even a term for it now: "gray divorce." And it is America's newest, dirty little secret about who lives at the poverty level in this country. Once again, it is women who pay the price for nurturing others. It is women who can't seem to get a free moment in life to simply trust that everything will always be okay.

So as sad as it is, I know that I will not be alone with my cat-food diet. But I do have a lot more experience with hard times, so that gives me a little bit of momentum. I know how to be alone. I know how to barely survive on very little. I am still thankful to be me instead of one of the married women who suddenly lost everything she thought she would always be.

While thinking about that, I realized that I have never known one single man in my life who I would want to hang around with for 30 or 40 years. Good grief, just the thought of it makes me gag. I get bored too easily. Bored with jobs, with routine. With men. I realize that I have never believed in that happily-ever-after dream.

I am perfectly okay now with saying out loud that I never saw anything amazing about married life. I am baffled by the fact that I continued to try it when I never liked it. How stupid it that? It's like making myself eat chicken livers every night for supper. Even though I hate them and have plenty of other choices in the kitchen, I might just force myself to eat chicken livers because everyone else likes them. So I decide that there must be something wrong with me since chicken livers make me throw up. Why did it take me so long to just be okay with me?

Yeah, hindsight can really kick your ass sometimes. I look back on all of my mistakes with much more maturity now. It is now too late in my life to fix most of those stupid moves. And I know that the rest of my years on this planet are not likely to be lived in a comfortable, peaceful manner. I feel very sad about that. But once again, it was my own doing. I have to take responsibility for all of the moments I lived like there was absolutely no tomorrow.

Here I am, a breast cancer survivor, so thankful to have a tomorrow. Maybe I should not take away from the joy I feel, just to be alive. And maybe I should just simply trust that God will always take care of all of us. Then again, maybe one day I will have to decide to develop a big old hankering for cat food. And if I do, I'll laugh about that, too, as often as I have the ability to make a devastating fact at least a little bit funny.

I will have plenty of company. There are many other women like me. We spent too many years trying to be loved, and we failed. On so many levels, we failed. But at the same time, we have lived colorful lives. There has to be some balance somewhere, right? Some balance between living on cat food but being okay with that because you are simply in love with life. And that cat food thing, well, that's just a little sidebar in the big story.

When I taste shame in my throat about the many ways I have failed, I hold on to a favorite quote by that beautiful soul, Maya Angelou: "When we know better, we do better."

Thank you, God, that I truly do know better now. And I just have to paste that thought across my heart.

I have accidentally made many, many mistakes in my life. Some of those mistakes were made out of hurt and fear. Others out of blind love. And others out of an incessant need to feel like I could have a happy ending that looked like a lot of other people's stories. Since breast cancer, I have tried harder to come to terms with the fact that my story has twists and turns and mountain climbs and moments of amazing adventures and accomplishments that are almost lost in the shuffle of deep, deep pain. My story is only mine. It is okay that it is punctuated with some regrets and disappointment. It is okay that I learned some things a little too late and others things far too early.

It is okay that some people in my life will likely always use my mistakes against me. Very often, those people strike out in an effort to avoid looking at themselves. But even that is alright. All of it is okay. I am trying as hard as I can try. And that's really all any of us can do.

September 2014

I couldn't think very well today. My work was moving slowly in my head, like it was bogged down in globs of heavy, unidentifiable gook.

And my back was killing me.

So I put on my two-piece bathing suit, grabbed my trusty old raft and walked over to the beach.

Except for a few people walking, that beautiful stretch of sand was quiet and private.

I walked out in the warm water and stared out at the blueness. I love that God made the sky different here. The blue is broader. The clouds are puffier. The water is forever.

I love how the beach constantly changes.

The tides change at different times. The same shells never wash up on the shore.

But even with those constant changes, I trust that the waves will come back.

Over and over again, they come back. It reminds me of breath and laughter and love, courage, hope.

I might think sometimes that laughter or comfort is lost forever in my life. But those experiences always come back. Just like the waves.

I don't know exactly why, but under the water, I took my top off. And I stared down at my implants.

There was a tan line on my chest, an old reminder of what I looked like with breasts.

Sometimes it feels like years ago that I lost my breasts. Sometimes it feels like it happened just yesterday. All I have been through during these months, all that I have learned, the symbol for all of those challenging moments is right here: these two cancer-free blobs on my chest.

They are constant reminders about how much you can learn and feel in the midst of a storm that takes place right in the middle of your soul.

I studied them, thinking.

Someday, when I have some extra money, I'll get the lotus tattoos and the quote. It will make this experience feel a little more finished.

During this nasty stuff of breast cancer, I lost so much but gained so much, too. In many ways, my life has blossomed in the last year. I have met such wonderful women because of breast cancer. I have taken an introspective journey through my heart and come out on the other side, willing to forgive myself instead of beating myself to death with old failures.

Next month, I will finally get to put my arms around my beautiful boy. One year and two months, I have waited and prayed for that. And next month, I will finally experience it. I hope not to start crying all over the place. Instead, I just want to hug him and feel like we just saw each other yesterday. For that moment, I just don't want breast cancer to steal my breath and darken the blessing of seeing my son again.

God, I am so very grateful to still be in the world. I am so, so grateful. I wish there were words to truly express how my heart fills up with joy and thankfulness.

It has been such a long trip through breast cancer. But I wouldn't change a thing. Not one thing. Every moment, good or bad, happens for a reason. I see many of those reasons. I am wiser and stronger because of where breast cancer has taken me.

It is weird that I can't feel my hands touching the implants. I remember what my own breasts felt like in my hands. But these flesh mounds have no sensation, no life to them. Because of them, I have life. And I am not as sad about how they look. My stomach doesn't jiggle anymore when I trace the scars with my fingertip.

Tears dripped down my face, but I smiled anyway as I held the implants under the water.

"You're not so bad," I said to the pretend boobs. "Let's hope we live a nice, long, peaceful life together."

Chapter Thirty-Five

After going through all kinds of hell for more than a year, I finally felt strong enough to travel.

That ability made me feel nearly normal again. It was early October. And I needed to see my son and my sweet little daughter-in-law. Every time I thought about putting my arms around them again, I was blinded by grateful tears.

I also had a long list of other wonderful people I wanted to visit. A book signing and comedy routine were scheduled, too. But the most important goal was to spend time with my son and daughter-in-law. I repeatedly told myself that I would not break down and cry all over the place during that long-awaited reunion. They could never grasp what I had been through in the last 14 months. I also didn't think they could understand what it would mean to me, just to lay eyes on them after all of so many months apart.

As soon as my son came into the world, I vowed to always be an attentive, understanding mommy. I promised him that he would always feel safe and loved. That we would never end a single day or telephone conversation without an "I love you." So until breast cancer, I have never been away from my child for a long length of time.

For months, I cried on my back porch on the beach because I missed him so much. I hated to be 1,200 miles away on his birthday. I hated so many things about the entire situation. At the time, I truly felt that I was protecting my son by not allowing him to see me in such a physical mess. Maybe I was protecting myself also. Avoiding a visit from my son during breast cancer treatment allowed me to continue the facade from his earliest childhood memory that his mama was strong and brave and immortal.

Maybe I wasn't ready for him to see weakness in my eyes. All I know is that when I knocked on their front door, my heart just kind of floated around joyfully in my chest. When my son opened the door, I moved right into his arms. Finally, my arms were around the person I love most in the world. I could take in a full breath. My face rested against the beating heart of my only child. I still had lots of life left. It was a salve for me, to just breathe him in and kiss his sweet face. I didn't want to let him go.

On the evening of my book signing, I was jittery. I had no idea how long I could sit up in a chair without shouting for pain pills. But my other problem was barely five feet tall. An older lady, who I happen to love so dearly, showed up unannounced. Suddenly, I couldn't do the routine I had practiced so carefully. She is in her eighties. She was married all of her adult life.

There is absolutely no way that she could ever grasp what the material was about. I didn't want to offend her or hurt her. So I didn't even do half of what I planned. I felt awful about short-changing the room full of women who are like me. Women who have survived divorce and raised kids alone. Women who have had their hearts repeatedly stomped. Women who cuss like crazy and laugh a little too loudly and sometimes get too rowdy. Those are the women who "get" me. They are strong and resilient, passionate and devoted to their children. They know how hard the world is on single parents. They don't judge. They are not conditional with their love. They are open-minded and tender hearted. But this older lady? She has never known that life. Going ahead with the material felt disrespectful. So I ended up disappointing bunches of other women in order to protect the feelings of one little lady, with her hair styled nicely, all dressed up and happy to see me.

After I had left the newspaper, she somehow got hold of my

phone number and called me. "I'm worried about you. Where are you now?" she asked. During that conversation, she also told me that she loves me. I happen to adore her. She is so kind to me and gentle. One evening, she invited me to eat supper with her. So we shared her delicious pan of cornbread and the rest of her great home-cooked meal and talked about all kinds of things.

Since I moved to Florida, she and I frequently traded handwritten letters and cards. There is nothing I would not do for this sweet woman. And I proved that at my book signing, by cancelling the stand-up comedy.

Unfortunately, I got a little bit too cocky or too anxious to feel like my old me. I overdid things on my trip north and pulled a muscle or something on my left side. I have a sneaking suspicion that repeatedly opening and closing the driver's door messed with my chest and my left arm. So I stopped driving myself anywhere, for fear of causing more damage.

That was such a disappointment, not to see all the friends, not to be mobile again. It was really hard on my heart. Saying goodbye to my son was at the top of the list for what was most difficult about that trip. Thank goodness that Elaine rode back to Florida with me. She ended up driving all of that first leg of the journey, which I felt awful about. She was worn out.

But I did not have full range of my left arm. Believe me, I was very grateful for her help. I would still be walking south without her! I was also relieved and thankful when my chest and arm finally stopped throbbing.

That's another something breast cancer often leaves with women: a healthy dose of paranoia. When something hurts, I no longer blow it off like I did for the first fifty-two years of my life. Before breast cancer, I decided that I was fine unless blood was spewing everywhere, my forehead was hot enough to fry an egg or a body part was turning green. Breast cancer stole away that lackadaisical attitude. Now I obsess about any little pain until I find some calm in the middle of the crazy shit.

I have no idea how many times I have had to remind myself that stinging and aching on my chest and upper arms have been part of my life now for over a year. Still, that knee-jerk reaction to a strange pain is, "Oh my God, is it back?"

That thought pattern makes absolutely no sense, of course. My right boob never let me know that it had cancer growing in the milk duct. My left one didn't send signals that it was messed up, either. Nothing hurt. Cancer was completely silent, which is even more terrifying. And so, intellectually, I am well aware of how silly it is to spend energy on instant worry and gloom. But I still do it. I can't seem to help it.

Another breast cancer survivor who also had bilateral mastectomy explained that losing breasts leaves a woman with the same symptoms other people sometimes suffer after a trauma, meaning that it is a lot like post-traumatic stress disorder. Many experiences during the testing, surgery and recovery are so painful, frightening and emotionally difficult to get through, of course you're bound to be at least a little bit of a nutcake. I think my friend is right about that. I am reminded of a dear friend who is a Vietnam veteran. In combat, he lost an eye and a leg. He always told me he could never forget an experience in his life that cost him body parts. He left those parts. When he initially shared those feelings with me, my heart was definitely touched by his pain. Now that I have been through all things pink, I very deeply understand what my friend was saying. I can't change clothes, get in the shower or bend over without being reminded that my breasts are gone.

Understand please that I am not at all comparing breast cancer survivors to soldiers. I am only pointing out the similarity of losing a piece of the body and the self. No matter how you lose that body part, it is definitely a strenuous and profoundly difficult situation to get through.

What a brave guy my friend is, with such a deep, rich heart. There are thousands more veterans exactly like him, just as there are thousands of women out there, with flat chests or implants, suffering and grieving about their lost breasts.

As the end of October rolled around, I spent a lot of time in the water. So nice and warm, it is like bath water. I have been drawn to the water for as long as I can remember. Even if it's too cold for me to take a dip, I just love to watch water. I love the sun sparkling on water. I love that water continuously moves and breathes somehow, like its own mysterious world. But, truth be told, I also had my hind end in that gulf water because I did not want to backslide again and be afraid to get in it. I didn't understand the anxiety I felt. I didn't know how to deal with it. Every time I went to the beach and got in the water without flipping out, I was pretty darn proud of myself. I finally beat that fear of putting my chest in the waves. At least one scary feeling was long gone.

Usually, that stretch of beach was deserted. So when I floated out there alone, I wasn't distracted by other people. I could spend a lot of time feeling more like my old self. And by the way, my old self was not nearly as much of a sissy as this new chick.

That fact bugged the hell out of me. Overcoming at least one of my weirdo fears made me feel better about myself. Though I still wrestled with sleeping in my bed and driving in the rain, I tried not to beat myself to death about it. I promised myself that I would conquer those problems just as I conquered the fear of the water touching my chest. I thought it would be kind of a break through, when I least expected it.

One day at the grocery store, I noticed orange and brown candy on the shelves. Time didn't register with me, for some reason. For days on end, I never thought about the months. I was focused on days and experiences. So I was surprised when I finally noticed that it was now late October. I am not a fan of Halloween. I loathe scary movies, scary stories, scary costumes. Scary anything. I probably delayed my son's social development by steering him away from utilizing fake blood and all of that yucky stuff as accessories for his Halloween costumes. I might be the only adult on the planet who knows absolutely nothing about those "Jason" movies and anything else that involves violence, neck biters or gigantic snakes. That is very likely the only part of my brain that is truly G-rated.

But I was curious about whether Halloween in Florida was different from Indiana, in any other way except the weather. I bought a big bag of candy, hoping the island children would come knocking. On Halloween night, I sat on the back porch, working, as usual, but also hoping that droves of little goblins would make their way up the porch steps. Not one little ghost showed her face. That was sad.

For a lot of the evening, I remembered that Halloween night is usually rainy, cold or both in Indiana. I envisioned little parades of costumed princesses and pirates, trudging through wet leaves on sidewalks and crowding around front doors of neighboring houses. Their trick-or-treat bags were open before a person appeared at the door. I remembered teaching my son about the season changes when he was maybe three years old. I pointed out the changing leaves, and his precious response was, "Mama, did God stay up all night, coloring those leaves?"

I missed Indiana. I missed the season changes. I missed my son. After Halloween, as we all know, the coming holidays are smooshed and smeared all over our faces. Retail giants have no shame. They don't mind at all to provide shoppers with yellow, brown and orange autumn-themed table clothes and paper goods, right beside bright red stockings and Santa hats. I was not excited at all about any of it. But on Thanksgiving Day, a friend and I drove out to Pine Island for a buffet dinner in a restaurant. Of course, the menu offered nothing emotional or family-oriented. The expectation was for diners to stuff their faces like sows and get the hell out, so new customers could have the tables. As I ate the meal, the turkey morphed into a huge dry ball in my throat. I felt sad and empty inside. My son and daughter-in-law were spending their day with my daughter-in-law's family. But there I sat, pretending to be over the moon about the sweet potatoes.

While I glanced across the room at older couples quietly sharing their meal, I thought about how much I love to cook for my boy. I thought about how happy I would be to get the hell out of the noisy restaurant. I wanted to be alone again in my pajamas. And I was also pissed off when I realized that I wouldn't enjoy leftovers for the next few days.

Chapter Thirty-Six

Barely recovered from the shallow Thanksgiving experience, I squinted at December 25 with dread in my throat.

I enjoyed Christmas most when my son was young. I loved to surprise him. I loved the way his sweet little face lit up when he bounced out of bed to see if Santa stopped by during the night. Since he grew up, I turned into a bit of a Grinch. I haven't had a tree for more than a decade. I don't decorate at all. I have always loved to buy gifts for other people. But it's a challenge to be excited about holiday shopping when you're not sure how you'll stretch the budget enough to also get the electric bill paid.

The good part about my situation was that I was back to working a lot of hours. That meant my dad no longer had to pay my bills. I didn't care how hard it was on me to financially find my footing again. And I still don't care. Nothing could be worse than knowing that my dad shelled out thousands of dollars for my medical bills, rent and everything else I needed. I could not stand the guilt and shame that went along with that. Plus, I felt like a huge loser. So I was perfectly fine with writing him a thank you note and letting him know that I wanted to take care of myself now. I felt much better about myself to be independent. I wanted my parents to enjoy their retirement and not feel responsible for me.

Being offered lots of December party invitations isn't fun if you don't have a companion. Very few single people of either gender will tell you they love to attend holiday parties as the Lone Ranger. In some ways, every party is the same; only the faces are different. One party has all the guys watching a sports event in the living room or they are in the designated man cave, playing pool and drinking beer while the women cluster in another area of the house. The other type of party has couples seated together, and the conversation is often "coupled," too.

Personally, I don't fit in well with either of those social arrangements. A lot of my single female friends feel the same way. It's not fun for a single, financially challenged woman to paste an obnoxious smile on her face and listen to married women talk about their winter cruise plans or the new recipes they want to try out for huge family gatherings. Single women — at least the majority of the single ones I know — can't plan a cruise since they are saving money to buy new car tires or pay the six-month car insurance premium. A huge family gathering isn't often the norm either in a single woman's home. If the kids are younger, they often spend half of a holiday with their father and his side of the family. If the kids are grown, they are busy creating traditions for their own little families.

And here's another FYI: We don't try out fancy recipes since we can't afford anything but basic condiments. This is not an exaggeration, you know. Many women in my age group live on less than $35,000 a year. If it's been awhile since you had to fend for yourself, imagine paying every bill alone every month while trying to put at least a little bit of that money in savings. There's very little left.

Yep, a single woman over fifty faces a lot more social and financial heartaches than she ever wants to discuss with a married woman. Now that I am older, I just refuse to put myself through the torture of showing up alone at a holiday party. I don't want to be around all the stuff that gives me instant diarrhea. Every single time I leave a majority married environment, I lie awake that night with that age-old question every single woman asks herself when times are tough: "God, what in the world is going to happen to me?"

So anyway, four days before Christmas, I celebrated my fifty-fifth birthday alone at the beach. Then my cousin Dayna very kindly invited me to spend Christmas day with her family. But I didn't want to intrude. She is married. Her kids are both married. I wasn't sure how I would fit. I tended more to think that I wouldn't fit at all. So I decided to volunteer instead at a homeless shelter. However, they never called me back about what time to be there.

The one something that has made me very happy for several Decembers is that I take my last one hundred dollars — I always make sure that I really need it — and then I randomly pick a person and give them my money. That moment is Christmas to me. Very often through the years, that moment has meant the most to me.

One year, I gave my hundred to a single mom at a dollar store, and she started hugging me and crying. Another time, I slipped it between the bills when I paid for gas. It is in that moment that I feel Christmas in my chest. But on this particular Christmas, I could not give away my one hundred dollars. Every single cent I had was already earmarked for bills. So I decided to delay my personal little Christmas tradition until I could get financially stable, or at least closer to it.

When Christmas Day arrived, I took a short walk through my neighborhood. When my chest stung every time I walked past a house where cars crowded the driveway or several family members enjoyed each other's company on front porches, I immediately changed my plan. I crossed the road and headed for the beach. Unfortunately, the sand did not provide the solace I was looking for, either. Actually I was shocked to see so many people on the beach. Not just people, mind you. Families. As I scanned the beach, my insides felt frozen. Once again, the realization of how deeply alone I felt crashed right into the moment of knowing how alone I really was.

I hurried home, shed the shorts and T-shirt for pajamas and did what I always do when I want to avoid pain: I buried myself in my work. That is how I survived two of the three divorces. I worked sixty-plus hours a week. I worked until I was too tired to think about pain. Too tired to feel it, too. By the time New Year's Eve arrived, I was ready to snort Prozac. No one was more happy than me to see the holidays pack up and get the hell out of Dodge for another calendar year.

I wanted to get back to whatever my new normal would turn out to be. But loneliness hung onto my heart. I was preoccupied with the pieces of my son's life that I was missing. I thought about my friends up north. I was mad at myself that, for some reason, I didn't have very many photographs of them. How could that happen? How could I love people so much but not have their photos? Well, I could answer my own question. I didn't have their photos because I took for granted that I would always be with them. I didn't have their photos because I had absolutely no idea what it would feel like to rarely see them anymore. Until it was too late, I had no idea how much I would have treasured pictures of us, cracking each other up.

The first year I lived in Florida, my son and daughter-in-law visited three or four times. I went north once. Since then, they visited only once. Soon into the start of my second year in Florida, my son was promoted at his job. His work hours increased, along with his stress level. Also, I didn't want him and my daughter-in-law to feel like they had to spend any vacation time they had with me. Then breast cancer came along and, as I said earlier, I nicely banned them from visiting me.

As the end of February rolled into view, less than a handful of potential employers had responded to the zillions of resumes I constantly sent out, trying desperately to find a job. I was digging a hole for myself that I would never be able to escape. One problem, at least in Southwest Florida, is that jobs are scarce. Also, if you are not in the medical field or the hospitality industry, you're dead in the water. Freelance jobs paid less than half of what I earned in Indiana, but with twice the work. Still on restriction, I could not lift more than five pounds and could not stand or sit for extended amounts of time. That little problem knocked me out of grabbing at a grocery checker job or even a server job in a restaurant, just to bring in a little more income.

Since I couldn't stand for an entire shift or lift groceries or restaurant trays loaded down with glasses, I figured I could not get a job at all unless somebody wanted to hire me to be a damn speed bump. My very stressful situation turned me into a walking facial tic. My years of journalism experience weren't scoring me any wins in area newsrooms, either. Novice reporters could be hired cheap and fresh off the college campus with a lot more technical skills than me. But I also doubted that I was physically ready to go back to working 15-hour days as necessary. I did not know what to do.

If I had had more time, I would have belly ached a lot more about how it felt to suddenly be put out to pasture by the next generation. But there was no time for whining. I knew I had to get busy finding at least one safety net — but preferably three or four, just in case one of those nets had invisible holes in it. After all, I have never had very good luck.

Completely on a whim, I threw some clothes in a bag on Easter weekend and decided to visit my son. I was sick of spending holidays alone. I was bothered by the fact that once again, time rolled right over me. Nearly seven months had gone by since I last saw my child. Deciding to surprise him, I didn't tell him or my daughter-in-law that I would be visiting.

Choosing Easter weekend for the big road trip was a stupid idea. A zillion drivers were on the road, pulling huge boats and nursing bad attitudes. In Atlanta, the rain poured after dark, which nearly resulted in a nervous breakdown. I don't see very well anymore to drive at night. The downpour, added to frequent accidents and unbelievable traffic made me nearly hysterical.

At the same time, my phone didn't work well. It barely rang when calls were coming through. Text messages were sometimes two or three days late. Long story short, I did not receive the frantic calls and text messages from my son and daughter-in-law. They noticed that, for several hours, I had not posted anything on Facebook. And I was not responding to their attempts to contact me since my phone was experiencing a slow death. When he finally reached me, my son said that I scared him to death. My apology barely made it out of my mouth since I felt terrible about alarming them. But I was also very hurt. Obviously, it was only meant to be a playful surprise. But it turned into my son being upset and me bawling for hours. No matter how shaky the hello happened to be, that April goodbye reiterated to me that I had to make some changes.

"I cannot do this anymore," I whispered to myself. "I just can't do it."

Thankfully, my friend Michele rode back to Florida with me. It was wonderful to have some company in the passenger seat. The 1,200 miles went faster on the ride home, too. Whenever you can laugh and talk with a girlfriend, anything is easier to get through. We only had a couple of days together before she had to fly back to Ohio, so we filled up the time with sun and sand.

Chapter Thirty-Seven

On the way to the plastic surgeon's office for my three-month check-up, those familiar stomach cramps made me break into a sweat. My throat was tight. My eyes burned. Yep, I now know a lot about anxiety. I also know a lot about how breast cancer and anxiety work together, to mess with my head.

When my name was called, I decided to just get it over with quickly, like yanking the Band-Aid instead of carefully removing it. I spilled my big fear. Lately, I experienced a new pain. I was scared to death of it. And every time I felt that new pain, I went a little bit bonkers with anxiety.

"My chest hurts when I bend over," I said to my sweet doctor. "It especially hurts on the left side. It feels like someone is trying to pull the implant off my chest."

By examining me she diagnosed the problem, and I learned about yet another possible way for breast cancer recovery to screw up the day. My left side was giving me problems because … wait for it … the implant had moved from the perfect little pocket on my chest where my real breasts grew. Yep, it just kind of jumped out of its designated pocket.

What?

Why?

And how could this problem be resolved? After all, I was slightly aggravated by the constant need to press on my chest with one hand so I could unload my grocery cart with the other hand. I was also tired of other shoppers staring at me with alarm on their faces, asking if I was suffering heart attack symptoms. But if I didn't hold my chest, it ached all damn day.

Scheduling another surgery was the answer I did not want to hear, to the problem I didn't even know to be possible. All of the incisions would be opened all over again. The new skin would be sewn and tucked tighter this time, so the implant had nowhere to go. I started shaking my head before her sentence found a period.

No.

Nope. I would not go through that. I was worn out from stress and worry, discomfort with the implants and pain from nerve endings still trying to find each other. Sometimes you just immediately know whether you can go through something or not. That moment, for me, at least, was crystal clear. I could not face a repeat surgery. I did not feel strong enough, not in any way at all, to face several more weeks of recovery, anxiety and pain. I didn't want to freak out for weeks on end, about whether my incisions would heal correctly without complications, such as infection. The doctor then reminded me once again that implant healing demands up to two years. There might be a possibility that my gypsy-hearted implant would go back to its address on its own.

I chose to hold my chest and put up with being asked if I was having "the big one." Three lengthy surgeries in four months had already toasted my brain. Being under anesthetic for seven to eight hours for each procedure had swiped a lot of what was in my head. Though my doctor promised that my memory would improve with time, I was six months past the last surgery and I saw no improvement. When I talked about the frustration and embarrassment attached to being unable to focus and remember very simple things, she then reminded me that some of the medication might be working against me. And of course, stress was again identified as a culprit. I blinked fast, trying to take control of those fat, hot tears that still drowned me at the drop of a hat.

Then I took a deep breath and told her that I was moving

north. She was the first person I told. But as soon as that announcement left my mouth, my throat filled up with a gooey mix of gratitude, fear and respect. How could I possibly thank her, for giving me the best she could possibly give during a time in life when my entire heart was shattered all over my scarred chest? How could I tell her how much she meant to me? How could I say that I would never, ever forget her kindness, especially on the day I completely lost my damn mind over the high blood pressure problems? I loved how she always entered the exam room with a big smile and a sweet "Hello, Miss Sherri."

I loved the times she reminded me that I was so strong. I remembered every single time she tried so hard to comfort me even though I didn't feel like holding my head up. She always told me that I could get through it. She always laughed at my silly humor, when I was trying to laugh instead of cry. When we hugged goodbye that day, I held onto her so tightly, praying that my heart would somehow transfer the gratitude I felt. Hoping that she would hear the words I could not say because by then, I was sobbing all over the place.

All the way home, I cried and cried. I cried because I was afraid to leave my doctors. I cried because I was afraid to move to Indiana. What if I failed there even more terribly than I failed in Florida, to get back on my feet after breast cancer? I cried because I would miss the beach. I cried because I needed a magic wand or a crystal ball. I needed a fairy godmother to rock my fifty-five-year-old ass on her lap and whisper over and over again that I could do this. That I could put my life back together and be happy someday, without constantly worrying about my future. I cried because I had friends in Florida who I loved so much. I cried because I was so incredibly tired of feeling like I was just jumping from rock to rock, hoping to find a place to land instead of falling even farther into this pit of anxiety.

A few days later, I started to pack boxes. That is very difficult to do when you can't lift more than five pounds. I ended up moving the boxes around with my feet, then asking friends and neighbors to stack them for me. Nearly every time I packed a box, I cried. I loved that sweet little beach house. I loved it with so much of my soul. I really did. And I loved my walks on the beach. I loved the memories I made there, laughing with new friends, meeting my neighbors, writing on that back porch until the sun poked through the trees.

Until I found that little cottage, I had never lived anywhere that I truly felt I was meant to be. I felt like I belonged in that little place, with the song the rain played on the roof, with the lizards and squirrels and birds. I was so grateful to finally experience that feeling, even if it was now time to let it go. Going through breast cancer in that innocent and spiritual little place was such a gift. As I packed my belongings, I tried to memorize every single something I loved about being there. I was fairly certain that once I left there, I would never again be in love with where I lived. I would return to perching, and feeling disconnected, with nowhere to lay roots. But that didn't change my circumstances.

"I can't stay here any longer," I said to God, too many times to count. "I will find myself under the beach bridge if I don't make a change. But I'm so afraid to go. Please help me to know that I am making the right decision. You know better than anyone that I sure can't afford to make one more bad choice."

A few days later, I saw my oncologist. As he examined me, I almost peed my pants. My right side started to throb. Amazingly enough, my right implant had also managed to abandon ship. By that point, I could do nothing else but laugh like an idiot. After all, the truth is always more funny than fiction. And my kitty heads listened and followed instructions just about as well as I did.

Late at night, I started to look at Indiana rental properties. I could be very happy in a cabin in the woods of Brown County. I could be very happy in a little house on the lake. But I knew those dreams were out of my reach. I still couldn't find employment in Indiana. I couldn't afford the extra gas money, to live so far away from any employment possibilities. I could not shovel snow anymore, due to my arthritic bones and joints. And what if I got stuck in snow or wrecked my car on ice, out there in the middle of nowhere? I had no one to help me.

But I still did the daydreaming. It was air to my chest, which grew tighter and tighter with worry and anxiety every time I packed a box.

When I saw my pain management doctor for my three-month check-up, it was again a very emotional goodbye. It was also difficult because she once again brought up the fact that she wanted me to at least try a medication for anxiety. In her opinion, my reserve tank was empty.

Medication would help take the edge off some of the stress I was facing. Medication would very likely help keep my blood pressure from whacking out. Medication would help control the muscle spasms in my back. So I finally gave in. I took the prescription to the pharmacy and swallowed it that first night, hoping that she was right. Maybe it would actually help me to get through the mountains of fear I felt I was now climbing every single day. It made me feel so very sad inside, to be this age, with nothing to hold onto that would always be mine.

My lease expired in late June. But my landlady said I could leave earlier if someone wanted to move in before time for me to officially move out. I knew it would be very hard for me to show my little baby house to someone new. It would make it more real to me that I truly had to leave it. However, I always choose to yank the Band-Aid. My things were in boxes. I was officially on my way back to living in limbo. I was tired of my heart hurting about leaving that house. My new thought was "Just get it over with now.

Get north. Do the best you can. Be with your son."

When a young couple stopped by one afternoon to see the house, I changed my mind about how hard it would be. In fact, it suddenly became more important for the new renters to be in love with that little house as much as I was. I wanted them to take care of it and love to be there, like I did. The moment I saw the young woman's eyes glow as she stepped inside, it hurt me like crazy. At the same time, I happily decided that I wanted her and her fiancé to have it.

"This is a special little house," I said to her. "I have loved every single day that I have been able to live here."

"I love it," she said happily.

"I can see that," I nodded, even though my eyes were full of tears. "Seeing that you will love being here makes it easier for me to leave it."

Two of my dear friends from high school made the trek south to move me back to Indiana. By then, I had finally surrendered to everything in my life that I could not fix or control. I could not find a job in Indiana. That meant I had no way to pay rent. So I secured a storage unit. I planned to couch hop at different friends' houses until I could find employment and save the money for damage deposits, etc.

I did not want to have to go through that. I did not want the extra stress of storing everything I owned and having no home. I had prayed and prayed for a job opportunity. But nothing materialized. My son assured me that I had a much better chance at finding a job in Indiana than I did in Southwest Florida. After all, I had spent countless months trying everything I knew to generate more income.

My son had never officially asked me to move back. But one day, we were talking on the phone about him and my daughter-in-law someday starting a family. And he said, "I just can't imagine us having a baby and you not being here."

His comment went straight to my heart and snuggled in there forever. I could not imagine that, either. I would not want to miss one day of watching my daughter-in-law carry a child. I would not want to miss anything about any part of that nine months. And I certainly could not picture myself 1,200 miles away from my grandbaby, either. When I felt so afraid that I could barely get my breath about the move, I replayed my son's comment in my head. I wanted more than anything in the world to witness that milestone in his life. I wanted more than anything to be the granny I have always dreamed about being. No matter how completely unraveled my life felt, there was another part of me that brought an immediate calm to my frayed nerves.

"I trust you, God," I frequently whispered. "I trust that you didn't bring me through breast cancer and some other very hurtful and damaging things this last year just so I could end up homeless."

The day that Brian, who lives in Indiana, and Michele, who lives in Ohio, started loading the truck, I broke down and cried. It was embarrassing. But when my belongings started to pile up inside that truck, it was more real to me than ever. I was leaving my baby beach house. I was blindly going back to Indiana, with no job and nowhere to live. My gift, however, was that I would be closer to my child. I absolutely could not stay in Florida without the financial freedom to see my son when I wanted to.

When some other friends, Tammy and Zach, stopped in to help with the packing, Tammy mentioned that her parents' home in Indiana was now empty. Renters had recently moved out.

It was amazing to me that in a matter of minutes, I had a place to land. Tammy's parents were so kind about helping me that they insisted that I not pay rent until August, so I had a chance to get on my feet. They also didn't charge me deposits.

"Oh my gosh, God, you rock," I whispered under my breath after finalizing that plan on the phone with Gary and Nellie. It always amazes me how God pulls things together at the very last minute. And so, because I suddenly had a place to go, I got more confident that a job opportunity would soon follow. I had almost five weeks to find a job after I got moved. I absolutely had to make that happen. Instead of being afraid of it, I just told myself that I had to pull it off. Had to.

The next morning, Brian crawled behind the wheel of the moving truck. Thanks to Suzanne, a fellow breast cancer survivor, and her husband Carl, I was able to get the moving truck at a greatly reduced price. My heart sometimes overflowed, knowing that so many people had gone so far out of their way to help me.

Brian and Michele had both taken off work to help me make this move. To say that I was grateful is such an understatement. I still have not found the right words to express to either of them, or to Suzanne, how much I appreciate all they have done. I also felt so grateful for another friend named Michelle, and her boyfriend Tony, for offering their home to me when I got back to Indiana. Those people and so many others rallied when I couldn't do anymore rallying on my own. Maybe they don't even know how close I was to the edge of not being able to take on one more crisis without cracking up completely.

Alone that morning, I walked over to the beach for the last time. Sobbing my heart out, I got on my knees in the water and buried a little something in the sand. I closed my eyes and thanked God for so many gifts: the chance to feel peace in a sweet little house, the treasure of walking on the sand and floating in the waves, the strength to survive so many challenges and the life I still had after breast cancer.

Very unexpectedly, a wave of absolute calm washed over me the moment I stood up again.

With my flip flops in my hand, I first stared up at the morning sky, wondering where that feeling came from and why. After all, I was definitely in a big mess. But for some reason, it didn't feel like such a mess anymore. I slowly walked back home, knowing that I was absolutely doing the right thing by loading up and going back north. Inside the now empty little house, I said goodbye to all of those wonderful feelings I experienced there. For the first time ever, I felt like I had a real home during the two years I lived there. I would always cherish that feeling. Even if I never captured it again, I was so thankful to know what it felt like to love being somewhere. Then I got in my car and slowly drove toward the island exit.

"Here we go," I said to God. "I have no idea what I am doing. But I'm just going to trust that it will all work out exactly as it is meant to be."

After a few miles of driving alone, Michele bopped out of the moving truck seat and climbed into my car. With the video option on my phone, we recorded the news that I was on my way back to Indiana and posted it on Facebook. I had told only a few friends and sworn them to secrecy. She and I laughed a lot, like we always do. And my heart never lost that new, brighter beat.

After the grueling, twenty-two hour drive, I unlocked the door of a little house I had never seen before and began to unpack boxes while other friends showed up to move furniture from the truck to the house and help me clean everything, too. Again, I was more thankful than words could express. I would never have been able to do all of that alone. And thankfully, I didn't have to try to find a way to get it all done. My friends showed up, just as they have for many years. And I could never say how deeply I love them for being there for me.

Though I thought about returning to journalism, I didn't feel confident that I could physically keep up. Plus, the doctor had told me repeatedly to do everything possible to avoid stress. But I didn't have any idea what was possible for me. Thankfully, God took care of that. Less than a week after moving in, I had a new job.

It is not just any job, either.

Initially, my job included some administrative tasks and marketing for a dear friend's funeral homes. For a long time, I have been very interested in this service for families. I became interested years ago, when I wrote so many stories about dying and grieving. But I had no idea how to even attempt to apply for employment since my knowledge of the industry was so limited. Those initial responsibilities, working for someone I respect very much, expanded to include an opportunity to become a funeral celebrant. This role involves meeting with families and helping them create a personal and beautifully healing service for their lost loved one.

I was instantly in love with this role and the many endless possibilities to make a meaningful difference in a family's broken heart. Less than a month after moving back to Indiana, I had a place to live, twenty minutes away from my son and daughter-in-law. I had an incredible new job, even though it is only part-time. My breast cancer book was finally done and ready for edits. And then I traveled to Memphis for five days to become a certified celebrant.

Now, here's the other amazing part. I live within walking distance of the funeral home where I work. All of those loose ends I could not manage to put together on my own have all been neatly tied into a knot by someone much bigger and brighter than me.

It is important to remember that blessings can always be found in the middle of the bad stuff of life. And it is also important to remember that many different sizes and shapes of miracles live in all things *pink*.

www.sherriconer.com